THE

ECONOMY OF BLISS

CORE VALUES

Stanlee E. Ngole

Copyright©2019
Stanlee E. Ngole
Contact: +237 698 796 883
+237 676 038 166
stanleengole@gmail.com
www.tenpercentafrica.org.

Cover design by *M. Media*

ISBN 9781798925850

Edited by **PATAMAE Research and Editing Consultancy**
paddyama@yahoo.com   (237)675959969

Economy of Bliss: Core Values — **Motivational**
1title 2019

Dedication

To Aren, my son, and to my parents, and to all humanitarian spirits, all people working to reduce the gap, all of them, directly or indirectly, partners and members of the *Tenpercent Africa Network.*

Acknowledgement

Mention must here be made of Mofor Charles, Ntoko Ray, Paul Metuge, Ngole Aline, Nkwame Adele, Ebasone Vanes, Ngufor Gil, Mande Melbourne, Messrs Ngome Blasius, Takere Nestor and Kwemain Roland who with many others, contributed in diverse and remarkable ways towards the realization of this work. I owe each one very personal and special appreciation.

"I alone cannot change the world. But I can cast a stone across the waters to create many ripples."

– Mother Teresa

Preface

In a world in which great wealth and extreme poverty mock each other in developed and developing countries, humankind seems determined to pursue the path of this continuous polarity that leads to its own destruction. The rich are not safe in the presence of the poor because the injustice or imbalance of their statuses leads to bloody revolutions. Most people ignore this very real and looming danger as they consider it the way the world runs, or probably the way it should be.

Ngole takes a step away from this thinking and looks keenly at the situation. He argues that it should not be that way and that there are alternative ways to reverse capitalism's dangerously high move towards revolutions. Capitalistic economy to him projects the misconception between riches and wealth. It is from this premise that he shows the way out, which is the economy of bliss, as he terms it.

The author's principled perception is developed in an exquisite two-part book. The first part is introduced with a broad survey of the grounds of our world of reality and perception. He refers to this as opening up the mind. Therein, he explores some ignored physiological realities of man. After bringing these to an explanatory correlation with the psycho-religious principles of balance, Ngole weighs in on the concept of social in/justice. From this well-explained relationship of the brain, mind and attitudes leading to social in/justice, he wisely proposes the way out in the second part: sharing values, gift economy and permaculture unto an economy of bliss.

He draws from recent technological advancements and research which indicate that human character is malleable and formed by experience, and that it can be forgotten or relearnt, thanks to the ability of the brain to form and re-organize connections.

Just as capitalism took over from another system, it too can and should be replaced. For, capitalism generates unhealthy practices like inequality, poverty and pollution; it is, overall, a dangerous system perpetrated by rigidity and an egoistic belief system.

It happens that the balancing tools of this dynamic equilibrium are virtues that include selflessness, gratitude and faith. These are elements or values of wealth rather than riches. This indicates a clear distinction between money, value and wealth. Ownership of money, including other external shows of riches, is an illusion, being part of the great misconception about possession at the expense of humanity and its spiritual potential.

Against the physicality of possessions comes the proposed new order which is the end point of this book. Stronger human relations, networking and a sharing economy based on shared values and altruistic thinking, expressed in such practices as the gift economy and in the environment-saving practice of say permaculture are thus proposed. These practices are seen to question such embraced social drawbacks as unemployment, fear, lack of business capital and poverty. Unemployment is mostly due to expectations of very small amounts of money, whereas true pay is not money but relationships and capacity. This clicks with the false notion that poverty is lack of money, whereas it should be lack of value, the latter being a rarer phenomenon. Capital too is often limited to money whereas the true capital is human value and skills, noticeably well spread among all people. But fear, besides holding the individual from venturing into great deeds, engenders malpractices like theft and lies. In all this, the evil hand of capitalist excessive reliance on money visibly raises the illusion of poverty, unemployment fraud, theft, and corruption.

Seen as the cause of much that is unwelcome, therefore, capitalism should give way to the new order abundance is generated and mental wellbeing and joy is secured by social balance or dynamic equilibrium, thanks to networking leading to an economy of bliss that should start with the reader and now.

Detailed and engaging in its tight logical flow, this book is characterized by deep keenness of thought and a disarming simplicity which is placed at the reach of anyone willing to follow the argument to the end. In this book, there are gems that strike the reader either by their novelty, ingenuity or plain commonsense. In my reading, whatever else can be ascribed to this discourse, it is true that, given the present realities of capitalist practices, this study cannot be ignored or gainsaid as it invites us to go beyond debates and blames of the current confusing situation to concrete and corrective action. We are to take it very seriously and start working to preemptively avoid the worst for mankind. The writing on the wall invites each and every one of us to take up the proffered option for an economy of bliss.

Roland Kwemain
(Chairman, Go Ahead Africa Ltd)

Contents

INTRODUCTION

When I was only a boy of about six years old, I had an experience that would determine the course of my life. In the first place, it can be said that I lacked nothing, for toys, clothes, sugary foods and television time were aplenty. Indeed, everything was mine for the need or the asking. Yet I was not for spoiling, considering that I received healthy doses of even spanks whenever my attitude asked for them. But even in this ambiance of balanced plenty, I felt that something was missing, a thing of extreme importance, a core factor in the life process.

I grew up with three sisters and an elder brother, and uncles and aunties always came and went over the years in succession typical of the extended family tradition. It was the kind of poise any unnoticed child has, seeing much, hearing much, but not being considered part of that reality. So, cat-like keen and quietly too, I observed everybody in what then looked to me like today's Big Brother shows. A child's heart goes with his senses so that beyond being observant, I was also particularly empathetic.

In front of my parents' house I sat, my feet in the drainage gutter, observing people and the child's little world. As the human beings walked up and downhill, I went in the shoes of some, wore their clothes, hijacked their thoughts and sank myself into what I imagined could be their own experience of life. My judgement could hardly matter then but it was obvious that many looked preoccupied, lost in thoughts of what didn't seem positive by the looks on their faces. And the child's sensitivity queued in as my spirits and moods often sank with what I saw or felt.

Some days it was strangers, people I did not know how they related to my family, that came to our house to ask for food. When my mom served them in the parlour, I would take cover as it were in my silent but close observatory. Besides noting their every physical move, I would get into their heads as it were. Questions snowballed but hung in the air about their status and how or why it was so permanent. Why, for example, did they have to beg from a strange fami-ly for food to eat? What was going on in their lives? What if they decided to attack us and steal or take away a share of all the privileges we enjoyed, rather than beg?

I did not understand the *system* by which we lived and I felt we were not really safe in a community where some people had more than enough and others had a hard time affording for themselves something as little as survival food. It was saddening and even depressive for me most of the time. My moods were soon compounded by mom who fell very sick and had to travel far off for treatment. Silent tears tended to invade my privacy and soon, I literally didn't like life; I couldn't understand it. How could I, when everybody seemed to have problems? Nobody seemed happy and when they expressed joy, it was punctually brief, an occasional respite in the general drama of pain, as I would hear it echoed by literature students. An existential worry pervaded my entire world view as I wondered why I was alive, why others were alive, what the point of everything was.

My fall-back stronghold was my family, my particularly compassionate mother, my eternally self-sacrificing, toiling dad who was constantly on his toes to feed our continually crowded house. And my dad, from all indications, loved his job. Mum and dad were the focus of my zoom lenses as I noted how they led their lives. They kept taking in more and more people under their care. They also kept climbing up the success ladder, which sparked a resolve in me, the decision that I was born to work hard and take care of other people too.

My parents took care of us all – children, uncles, aunties, grandparents, cousins and many strangers at the time. It was a relay baton of care we had to take up. We had to grow up also and take care of other people, if we had to be as successful as mom and dad were. And in our attitudinal choice, the nuance of success as work and service was already somehow crudely registered.

On hindsight, I think that period of my life shaped everything for good: I didn't want to do anything that would hold me back from helping the world on my own terms. I instinctively knew that I could not be happy or self-fulfilled otherwise. My choice of entrepreneurship along with personal development coaching as against full employment and the job security of civil service is the marker.

Somewhere behind these life choices of mine was a drive for positive change in the way people live. I wanted to pull out a long-ignored stone from inside their shoes. I realized that a lot of people suffered because they missed out on an essential point about life. That vital but missed part is what is found in this book, a central theme and mission of my non-profit enterprise, the *Tenpercent Africa Organization*.

Like life, this mission is founded on the profound existential basis, representing unsolved mysteries from the beginning of time. Dozens of theories have been advanced in the course of human history in a bid to explain the nature and meaning of life. Some are scientific, some religious, some intuitive, and yet others are processed in objective, critical and philosophical reasoning. Among these can be found the extreme stance, for example, that life has no meaning (nihilism), a perspective boosted by an even more extreme argument – *anti-natalism,* which holds that it is an immoral or an evil act to bring people into existence and hence to harm.

The South African philosopher and author, David Benatar (2006, 18-59), argues in *Better Never to Have Been* that coming into existence is a serious harm for sentient beings, regardless of their feelings or emotions, once they are born. To him, life is worse than inexistence because even what may be perceived as momentary pleasures therein are not real advantages, compared to a state of inexistence.

The tickle of experience perhaps makes us shudder at David Benatar's view, and each of us can draw our conclusions on it. Yet, the perception seems to be vindicated by suicide rates. That notwithstanding, relatively few people would want to snap out of existence. However, even fewer people would disagree with the notion that life is a tough and challenging experience. For this challenge, everybody is constantly seeking solutions – a better life for themselves and those they love. It is everyone's concern then. Can we then, together, sustainably satisfy these desires and increase the quality of our lives?

From ancient times, but in recent times particularly, it is the hyped buzz that our species thrives in networks of all kinds. We strive to build communities of different forms of parasitic and symbiotic relationships in order to obtain the values needed to make us get the best out of our lives.

Being highly complex beings, the quality and survival of our relationships depend to a grander extent on the net value that each party obtains from the constructed communities. When we feel as if we are giving value in one relationship but receiving less in return, we naturally get distracted from the said relationship by those in which the value derived is relatively greater. Alternatively, we become hostile and repulsive towards the unproductive party.

Those who obtain useful value from a relationship, whether they invest relevant value into it or not, tend to hold on to the relationship and *wish* for it to stay alive. This applies to relationships between individuals and those between entire bodies, including nations, collectives of different races and tribes. The horrendous deterioration of relations between the Tutsi and the Hutu tribes of Rwanda into the soul-wrenching genocide of 1994 is a stark exposure of the extent of damage that dissatisfaction can cause.

The relationship between the poor and the rich in every community should be considered to be in urgent need of attention. The abundance of both peaceful and violent manifestations by poor communities around the world results from extreme inequality. And this is a fear that even a child (as happened in my six-year-old childhood dread above) can nurse but which, perhaps, grownups are not sensitive enough to. The relationship between these two classes or communities keeps deteriorating.

The extent to which the frustration of the poor can stretch will certainly not be checked by charlatanistic politics of hollow promises. Preventive laws and military power are no use either. Genuine humanitarian diplomacy, an increased sense of social justice in more and more people, translated into a widespread sense of collective social responsibility seems the only viable solution.

There is a range of balance in all things whose disruption causes disaster, brought on by forces of any kind. A car driven without servicing works normal until it breaks down at one point, sometimes beyond repair. Careful drivers service their vehicles regularly to ensure this balance. Relationships too require servicing to be maintained in a state of balance. Governments hire the best diplomats for this; companies hire Public Relations experts, and individuals study interpersonal skills to the same effect.

A system designed to reward the extremely rich and powerful, causes a constant and widening gap between the rich and the poor. There is no way the relationship between these two groups can be kept from deteriorating in such a set-up. The salvific move is the answer to the following questions: What are the effective mechanisms that can promote the development and integration of poorer communities into society? How can existing mechanisms be made better?

Because human perception is characterized by ranges, the question of *who is rich and who is poor* should pop up here. To that, a pragmatic definition is in place as guide to what is meant, to wit: the *rich* are those who control significant chunks of a nation's wealth. Since they are very few, the chances are that you are not one of them. But you are not poor either, so long as you're capable of giving value in any form, to better the life of someone else, even for a minute. Collectively, we are rich, therefore. If those at the bottom can come together as one, the pyramid will be forced to stand on its head and narrow down to a trapezium. In this light, this book is for everyone to read and act upon.

If happiness and abundance in every area of life could be taken like a pill, everyone would want to have an overdose of it. The success of the *Law of Attraction industry* is a reflection of this reality. While we might agree that all people can never live together in perfect harmony and have everything they desire, it is also true that, imperatively, an aspect of happy living and balanced relationships is missed by perhaps a majority of people. Tirelessly, most people work in a day after day humdrum to earn a salary at the end of the month or make a profit of some measure, to be able to sustain themselves in an environment of perpetual want. The benefits of our work in the guise of direct profit, proceeds or salary we so devoutly pamper, that some organizations and individuals resort to manslaughter to protect pecuniary interests.

On deeper consideration, one observes that the true guarantors of the comfort of the *rich* are the *poor*. If the *poor* fought back collectively, the *rich* would be in trouble. This highlights the point of Aristotle's one-liner to the effect that *poverty is the parent of revolution and crime.* As a philosopher, he put his thumb on the point. The materially rich, or those who own any property at all, must be on the perpetual watch out, aware of the possibility, in some dark corner of their minds, that they are not safe in the midst of people who lack basic needs. This stirs insecure feelings as we all run the same perpetual risk of losing all our wealth and even lives, if a war were to break out in our country, for example. In the event of conflict, not even the poor are safe, but the rich have more to lose in such an eventuality.

It stands to reason that those who would be quick to take to the streets with arms, should social and economic decay call for it, are the poor. They would not hesitate to bring down buildings and incinerate property, things they regard as proof of economic injustice but which, to their owners, are but the fruit of their sweaty struggles. Who compensates for the damages at the end? Optimism does not require one to ignore the negative side of things. Cognizance of these negative possibilities should be taken along with contemplation of ways to mitigate them. This is the means to maximize the chances of sustaining a positive outcome.

How then can our collective moral and material wealth be preserved from the dangers of extreme inequality? How then can we make the poor feel worthier of humanity and stay creative rather than destructive in the process of getting a better life? How can more wealth be created without the poor increasing in number or suffering further relegation?

This book aims at adding greater value to your life, whether you consider yourself rich or poor. In it is a smart perspective on how to enrich your experience of life, become wealthier, experience more love, feel more secure in your community and live happier. Enjoy your read!

PART ONE

CHAPTER ONE

OPENING YOUR MIND

How our minds work and what causes us to do things the way we do is a relevant introduction to how the world works and how to make it better from our individual viewpoints. Our personal beliefs on what life is all about are each correct from their various source perspectives. However, we should be alerted to the fact that even belief systems have a system by which they operate, and that our knowledge of this fact is vital to attaining our full potential as creative beings.

The Biology of Belief

Beyond personal convictions and religious beliefs, great strides have been made in modern science towards understanding human nature and determining whether we are all part of some greater purpose or are merely experiencing the effects of our own thoughts and actions. Until the late 20th century, it was accepted as a hardly challengeable fact that the human brain was hardwired or operating with predetermined genetic configurations. This belief was supported by scientific studies that employed research techniques and facilities then available. Emotions and behaviours were considered to be determined by individual genetic configurations.

Recent advancements in technology and research amenities have led to the relegation of these earlier perceptions. It is now considered indisputable that everything we refer to as character or behaviour is learned, can be forgotten, and can be relearned. The constituents of the person – character, likes, dislikes, hobbies, passions, beliefs and doubts – result from life experiences had or from direct education. We are educated by the places, information and experiences we are exposed to.

Thus, children born and bred in remote villages in Africa, where there are no formal pedagogic institutions, will have different knowledge and abilities from those born and raised in city centres and given formal education. Those born and bred in North Africa or Saudi Arabia, with the prevailing culture there, would be Muslim while those raised in Europe or the United States would more likely be Christian. These broad examples, of course, can filter in to the minutiae of attitudes, likes, dislikes and mannerisms.

Neuroplasticity

Plainly, if we expose ourselves to other cultures and beliefs by various means, aspects of our identity as well as the opinions we hold are likely to change, irrespective of the belief system or culture we already have. The brain is not hardwired but equipped with an amazing functional element known as neuroplasticity, the discovery of which has taken us above and beyond the *nature versus nurture* debate of old. This revolutionary knowledge brings to the fore the reality that we basically nurture our nature. True, this is done over time by the experiences we get. A constant state of dynamic interaction between our brains and the world ensures this. For, although everything we do comes from our thoughts, the nature of the brain is influenced or rewired continually by our experiences. Simply understood, therefore, our beliefs and habits are not really "us". They are only a reflection of the various things which have seeped into our subconscious, the influences we have had over the years.

In the brain, scores of billions of neurons keep firing impulses in teams depending on the nature of the activity they are coordinating. It works this way, for example: if you have never played the guitar before, your first attempt at learning will have you connect new teams of up to ten thousand neurons that may never have communicated or interacted in the past, including neurons that might not have been put to use before, but which exist idly in the brain. These fresh and new neural connections will struggle to get "used to" each other as you progress in learning to play the guitar until they give a new configuration to the brain. Soon there is configured a *new brain which also knows how to play the guitar* through the process known as *long-term potentiation.* Configurations and reconfigurations occur in this manner each time we encounter new experiences or learn new things, thanks to the brain's neuroplasticity.

Belief Systems and Worldviews

Sam Bartram the English professional goalkeeper, stayed 'catching' on the pitch some 20 minutes after the match had ended. Let us consider his story as recorded in his autobiography.

'Soon after the kick-off, fog began to thicken rapidly at the far end, travelling past Vic Woodley in the Chelsea goal and rolling steadily towards me. The referee stopped the game, and then, as visibility became clearer, restarted it. We were on top at this time, and I saw fewer and fewer figures as we attacked steadily.

The game went unusually silent but Sam remained at his post, peering into the thickening fog from the edge of the penalty area. And he wondered why the play was not coming his way.

After a long time, a figure loomed out of the curtain of fog in front of me. It was a policeman, and he gaped at me incredulously. "What on earth are you doing here?" he gasped. "The game was stopped a quarter of an hour ago. The field's completely empty".'

At the risk of an oversimplified overgeneralization, I placed this story here to vivify the following questions: *What if the match you are playing was already ended long ago and you're just not **aware** of it yet? What if your belief system is limiting and helping you only to waste your time?* Perhaps a little further probe into the concept of belief systems vis-à-vis the brain's function would be in place here.

The neuroplastic abilities of the brain shelter belief systems and engender what can bc referred to as *auto-*

piloting or worldview. This inertia or *auto-piloting* stasis comprises all the information you hold as true at any point in time and by which you lead your life; it is the total sum of the information in your mind, which influences your thoughts, choices, behaviours, fears and beliefs. Everybody has a unique belief system, representing their whole personality, and it is impossible to function without one. From place to place, person to person and community to community, belief systems vary in quality and permeability.

This variability means that some people and groups would be more or less rigid than others. The less rigid ones tend to be more open-minded, more likely to entertain ideas that go contrary to their beliefs. Of course, this does not mean that they easily switch to new courses but that they allow these new turns to play along with and into their worldview. The more rigid holders of belief systems are less likely to entertain any belief contrary to their preregistered ideas, which to them is a kind of security hold. We leave out the possibility of malice as well although they may even turn hostile in cognitive dissonance when faced with such differing notions.

Extreme rigidity in belief systems is what may cause a devout but sick Amish to reject all forms of modern medical intervention, or, for that matter, a typical Cameroonian youth to prefer spending substantial amounts of money trying to enrol into the civil service payroll rather than starting an entrepreneurial adventure. If Sam Bartram, in our story above, were to argue with the policeman and mock him rather than allow himself to see that he was the only player left on the pitch, we would consider it absurd.

For all that may be considered outlandish or faulty in the stasis of belief systems, it is a potent value. The reason is that, without the purposive and directive property of belief systems, people would hardly pursue any creative ambition, life would be a senseless and chaotic interplay of random events in succession. Belief systems therefore give a context and orientation in the way things are done. It is a compass as it were, and should serve as the kick-off point for human adventures into other possibilities. The snag is when it is held to blind alley inelasticity.

Sam Bartram's belief system is what kept him on the pitch. In the absence of that belief, he might have left the pitch before the end of the match and perhaps conceded a goal from his opponents. So, belief systems are important, whatever their nature, but they can and should be changed or modified when need be in order to improve on the quality of individual or community life. There is need for continual openness to new and better parameters. As with computer programs, for an individual to attain full potential, their belief systems must be permeable enough to allow for updates in the form of new information to enhance existing information and replace obsolete ones.

Every aspect of the world, to a great extent, reflects or is the effect of collective belief systems. The outbreak of the First World War in 1914 exemplified this. Out of their need for gold to finance the war, the British government and the Bank of England convinced the British people through media propaganda that it was unpatriotic to redeem paper money for gold specie. This marked the end of the gold specie and a series of later events led the world to adopt the FIAT-money-based capitalist system, which prevails globally today. A singular belief can pool up with similar beliefs from thousands of people to create a reality out of nothing. This clarifies why, despite the extreme inequality, extreme poverty, pollution and unimpeachable evidence around the world that capitalism is a dangerous economic system for humankind, fear-ridden, rigid and egotistic belief systems continue to hold it in place. A new, unfamiliar system of living, such as the gift economy, permaculture and creating shared value may erupt cognitive dissonance in the minds of people who have known only capitalism in their lifetimes and, as usual, their resistance would be made manifest in stiff resistance or even violent aggression to change.

Cognitive Dissonance

As the expression goes, cognitive dissonance is discord or discomfort associated with holding two or more contradictory beliefs at the same time, or a reaction to being presented with a perspective that does not match one's current knowledge. My favourite illustration of this phenomenon is in Plato's allegory of the cave, which illustrates human perception and the effect of belief systems and cognitive dissonance on people. Slightly different variations of this story have been told and retold over time, but, centrally, it is the same:

In a dark cave, three prisoners are tied up from birth and cannot see anything except the stonewall before them; they do not even see each other. Behind them is a raised walkway out of the cave. Further away, there is another raised wall on which there is a fire. People walk along the walkway between the stonewall and the fire, carrying on their heads objects like rocks, domestic animals, wood and plants. They also make noises. As they move, the fire above them casts the shadows of the objects they are carrying on the stonewall, and the prisoners can see these shadows but not any of the objects which are borne by the people behind them. The prisoners believe these shadows to be the "real" things.

Later on, one prisoner breaks his chains and on turning, sees the fire. It dazzles him at first, but he goes on and walks up and out of the cave into the open. There he discovers people and things and is further dazzled by the bright sunlight. He realizes that his previous notion of reality was very limited and, good man, he returns to the cave to free his mates to share his newfound experience. When he gets there, he finds himself 'blind' for he once could 'see clearly' in the darkness of the cave, but now back from the 'outside' dazzle of sunlight, he can no longer see. When he attempts to free them, they threaten to kill him, for fear of becoming 'blind' like him. On account of the cognitive dissonance in them, they become hostile towards the freed prisoner. He had returned with ideas which did not match their belief system and so they rejected them as nonsense.

Like these prisoners, many are stuck, their faces to the wall, closing themselves up to new ideas and modes of thought, even condemning them by labelling them with various hateful names. Their only explanation is that the said ideas do not fit the views with which they have been brought up. So, they are stuck in linear lives of strict doctrines and very limited knowledge of the beautifully complex world in which we live. They live inside what has been termed 'the box'.

A minority of people, who might be labelled 'freethinkers', cultivate a sincerity in which they hold non-binary or other non-rigid labels. They hardly feel the need to cluster within exclusivist aesthetic or dogmatic classifications like black/white, Christian/Buddhist, or CPDM/SDF. Granted, some may label themselves with the objective of blending in society. Also, it is not that they do not have preferences and opinions, but they rather often prefer the grey zones, from which position they are usually excited to entertain other people's beliefs and opinions. In social circles, these grey zone indigenes are usually the opinion leaders, their mental flexibility and open-mindedness making them inclusive rallying points. This category of people is better able to pursue critical thinking and settle on sound judgement. They push to the limits of possibilities and model the world by their imagination.

CHAPTER TWO

NATURE'S OPERATING SYSTEMS

While it might seem a wild conjecture to insinuate that nature is run on an operating system, there is enough in social assumptions to make this not so outlandish. For one thing, many share in the belief that God runs the world, deciding what should or should not happen in it. That perception leads to the question of the very

> *God doesn't play dice with the universe.* **– Albert Einstein.**

nature of God, a divine person, a spirit like the spirits which inhabit us all, men like women. The variety of experiences, ideas and opinions around, however, lead to much speculation on this matter. What stays unquestionably steady is the evidence of laws in nature by which everything in it operates. These laws interlock into systems and operate in closed cycles that know no waste.

When I eat an orange and throw its seeds out the window, for example, the seeds either germinate to form new orange trees or rot into organic waste to fertilize the soil for other plants to grow and be eaten by animals and people. The other alternative is that the new plants or fruits get crushed to dusty habitats or bacterial vectors. Nothing becomes nothing; nothing is wasted. By this cyclic quality of nature our species subsist on earth. It is visible all around us: fossil fuel deposits from thousands of years ago are mined today as diamonds and other minerals.

According to the law of energy conservation, energy can neither be created nor destroyed in an isolated system. This implies that all energy once exerted, must be harnessed somehow. Yet, human methods violate these closed cycle systems in innumerable ways, including overproduction, excessive production of inorganic materials, greed and materialism.

The law of indestructability also applies to emotional energy. When we are greedy and wicked, we emit psychic energy that is perceived by those around us and harnessed to become resentment, for the most part. When we express generosity and love, on the other hand, the reaction of our surroundings is more positive; we attract the energy of other people towards ourselves. This can be renamed the law of causality, one of the systems by which nature operates and by which one thing must lead to another.

Thus, by this law of energy conservation, the amount of energy in a closed system remains static, neither increasing nor reducing although transferrable from location to location as well as alterable in form and quality. A dynamic equilibrium is this way ensured, a balance that maintains justice in nature, and to which we are all subject. A closer look is in place here under the sub-titular shadings of *Causality, Dynamic Equilibrium, Perfection of All things, Magic in Everyday Life,* capped by *Some Balancing Principles* and the story of *my encounter with Prince.*

Causality

One thing leads to another in nature so that even the tiniest actions can lead to remarkable effects as in the following anonymous story.

"Choices made, whether bad or good, follow you forever and affect everyone in their path one way or another."
– J.E.B. Spredemann

Mark was walking home from school one day when he noticed the boy ahead of him had tripped and dropped all the books he was carrying, besides two sweaters, a baseball bat, a glove and a small tape recorder. Mark knelt down and helped the boy pick up the scattered articles. Since they were going the same way, he helped the lad with part of the burden. As they walked, Mark learnt that the boy was called Bill, that he loved video games, baseball and history, and was having lots of trouble with his other subjects. In addition, the boy had just broken up with his girlfriend.

They arrived at Bill's home first and Mark was invited in for a drink and to watch some television. The afternoon passed pleasantly with a few laughs and some shared small talk, then Mark went home.

They continued to see each other around school, had lunch together a few times, and then graduated from junior high school. They ended up in the same high school where they had brief contacts over the years.

Finally, the long-awaited senior year came and three weeks before graduation, Bill asked Mark if they could talk. Bill reminded him of the day, years before, when they first met. "Did you ever wonder why I was carrying so many things home that day?" he asked. "You see, I cleaned out my locker because I didn't want to leave a mess for anyone else. I had stored away some of my mother's sleeping pills and I was going home to commit suicide. But after we spent some time together talking and laughing, I realized that if I had killed myself, I would have missed that time and so many others that might follow. So you see, Mark, when you picked up those books that day, you did a lot more, you saved my life."

The story speaks for itself, illustrating *causality*, the philosophical principle that every change is produced by some cause. Indeed, the principle is all over: every occurrence or action is produced by a prior occurrence or action of some nature or by an entity or an interplay of entities. The prior action could be passive or active, an action or an inaction; either is a valid cause of change. The absence of action (omission) can permit an occurrence to happen. Thus, silence and speech each have their consequences.

Since we act from particular perspectives, worldviews or beliefs, our collective beliefs, emotions and reasoning, or their absences, are the cause source. Every action we undertake has an effect or a consequence, and each effect leads to another effect to form an unending chain of occurrences whose overall impact we naturally tend to underestimate, or ignore, since it is difficult to take stock of long stretches of happenings. This interplay of successive life occurrences, where current events depend on past and other current events, form what is known as the *causal system*.

A career-oriented student who doesn't perform well at school may later have difficulties integrating the job market. One who excels at school, on the other hand, likely finds a job with less struggle. Assuming that formal education measures intelligence and competence, a drop in the average performance of the students should be echoed by a drop in the performance of the companies that employ them, and vice versa. The principle of causality on its own, however, would be chaotic if it operated without the participation of another mechanism to balance it – *dynamic equilibrium*.

Dynamic Equilibrium

The state of balance between continuing processes make up what is here labelled *dynamic equilibrium*, a concept which

> *There exists everywhere a medium in things, determined by equilibrium.*
> – Dmitri Mendeleev

has been used in various disciplines to express balance of some sort among opposing forces in a system. In nature, as in life in general, the principle is at work in countless ways. Socially, the principle is checked to prevent *causational chaos* in which reactions would succeed actions without reasoned wavering. Socially, for example, an apology is a checking mechanism. For, if you are hurt by someone, causality on its own would have you get mad at them, revenge or take up any retaliatory action. But you hold back by ignoring the pain or accepting a plea for forgiveness. This way, you check the causality chain and restore a state of balance in your relationship with the cause of your hurt. Thus, you can choose to absorb the energy exerted on you and transform it, rather than mirror it in return.

The dynamic equilibrium principle in the global ecosystem ensures that expense in energy be replaced by its equivalent. The sun's rays heat up the earth's surface and vaporizes water into hot air, which continues rising into the atmosphere until it gets too dense and tumbles down as water droplets or rain. Rain in turn waters crops to enhance food growth. We harvest and eat the food that powers our activities and our bodies produce excrement that is recycled into earth to moisten solids and chemical components for the complex cycles to spin on. Amidst all these convection currents, dynamic equilibrium is causally at work with life itself remaining constant as the human race and all other living things are kept alive.

Dynamic equilibrium is played over in practically everything, from human relationships, through natural disasters, to species evolution. The institution of marriage, where two complex beings unite in a constant state of complementarity illustrates this too. When this complementarity or equilibrium is not well maintained, disequilibrium becomes visible in fighting, bitterness and even divorce. In the process of evolution, dynamic equilibrium allows species to naturally develop new features and lose others, to adapt to their environment and maintain the constant, which is life on earth.

Analysis of societal scenarios emphasize the fact that the laws of ultimate balance and causality are central to systems. Given that equilibrium is in part determined by the nature of the policies of leaders, disequilibrium may occur when populations become dissatisfied with the said policies. If complaints are not addressed, disequilibrium will set in and build up, unless it is checked by an effective and collaborative effort of both sides to restore equilibrium.

In romantic or other human interactions, dynamic equilibrium is maintained by the mutual considerations of the parties. In this respect, honesty earns trust and maintains the relationship, while cheating deceitfulness topples it to imbalance. It would seem that, in human relationships, equilibrium is pitched on love and tolerance among other values, the absence of which creates and maintains failure of relationships. "Natural man, in order to preserve life, must seek peace," wrote the English philosopher, Thomas Hobbes, obviously in the mind-set of dynamic equilibrium. It is obvious therefore that the interplay of causality and dynamic equilibrium is the primitive process by which all things are made perfect.

Perfection in All Things

The idea of a just and perfect world may sound strange to many, given the abounding suffering, injustice and crime in the world. Hard a concept as it is, considered from another angle, it is valid. Charles Swindoll declares that "Life is 10% what happens to me and 90% how I react to it". Having the freedom to choose, human beings have control over their reactions to circumstances, welcome or unwelcome. How we use this power of choice vis-à-vis the energy which the world directs to us determines our fate. Our total control over our attitudes or reactions is precisely what makes life fair and just.

A little search would bring up a host of people who have overcome unbelievable adversity and risen beyond heights anyone would have imagined before. At the risk of sounding parochial, one of such people is my father, one perfect example of somebody who braved hardship and faced a visibly negative life with a positive attitude. Born into a very poor family in one of the remote villages, he rose through excelling at school and winning multiple scholarships to eventually peak in his service, emerging as a top-ranking official in the government of Cameroon. His success story can be fitted in the lives of many other people, if we take the care to look around us. For quite a handful of people have understood that life is fair to the measure that we believe it to be.

We can pick on the world figure, Nelson Mandela, who was oppressed and imprisoned. His twenty-eight years in prison rather helped him to build the momentum to later rise to power as president of his country and to reconstruct the deteriorated South African society.

A multitude of people born with 'golden spoons in their mouths', on the other hand, end up nowhere close to being successful at the individual level, but become unhappy, unfulfilled, dissatisfied, or simply cut, the sorry figure of failure and underachievement. Their comparative start-off advantage does not seem to be of any good to them.

Your current situation is thanks to the choices you have made and your future is dependent on today's attitude towards people and situations. Dynamic equilibrium dictates that once you take responsibility for the present, you ensure balance in your life and expose yourself to opportunities to flourish. But if you become bitter about life and shift blame for your unwanted circumstances to someone or something else, whipping up sentiments of victimization and powerlessness, you upset the balance of dynamic equilibrium; you fail to plant your seeds of success and water them by surrendering yourself to the buffets of natural selection and thereby to be eroded by the forces of nature.

Much depends on the individual then. It does no good to shift blames for undesirable situations to the government, bad weather, life, X's incompetence or Y's negligence. For in so doing, you give up on your power to shape the future; you lose the advantage of taking up and using your responsibility for the present.

The dynamics so elaborated, boil down to the fact that everything is energy. The thoughts we think, the words we speak and the emotions we entertain, all carry energy. And as already said, energy can neither be created nor destroyed but only transformed from one state to another. The idea of 'positive and negative energy which has made their rounds of popular culture, should simply mean energy and neither positive nor negative. What you choose to do with your energy qualifies it as either positive or negative; this is elaborated later below where we show how magic works.

When you interact with people, you exchange energy which builds up or destroys you. When you meet someone for the first time and who does not return your smile, for example, you decide on whether to keep a positive image of the person, giving them the benefit of doubt, or to build a negative image of them in your mind and go on with it. Your own decision determines your fate relative to that person. By the same token, if you oppress people, you build energy in them which they can use as they choose, thus creating precariousness for you and momentum for the oppressed to flourish as in the Nelson Mandela example. This principle is what inspired the mafia rule that *people problems must be dealt with harshly*; you either crush your target completely or do not do anything at all.

A worrisome truth, too, is that good people die from oppression by others. The question arises whether death is a bad thing. Considered as the access route to a higher existential state, death does not seem to be bad. As the French Jesuit priest and philosopher, Pierre Teilhard De Chardin says, "we are not human beings having a spiritual experience, we are spiritual beings having a human experience". As spirit beings, we are born into the world with the mission to create experiences and participate in the universal creative process. Our effectiveness depends on the extent to which we take responsibility for our actions. Of course, we need to protect our environment rather than harm it. If we fail in this, the law of natural selection takes us out, for failing to maintain universal dynamic equilibrium. And where even external balancing is not obvious, the human conscience has a powerful balancing ability. It can silently punish even the most successful tyrants in ways that *others* may never know.

Reduced to a containable and practical slice of fact, when you wake up from sleep every day, you wake to the choice of whether to affect or be affected by your world. You may suffer injustices but how you react to them is what determines your fate. It is your free choice, your conscious power to influence causality and determine prevailing states of dynamic equilibrium. It is the representation of the potential state of perfection in the world and depends on our individual course of action and reaction, on the things we do, the way we act or react towards our experiences. The free energy in nature, has no conscious intention but we can harness it for whichever purposes we choose. Thus, while the energy we encounter everywhere around us is neither positive nor negative on its own, how we receive it or react to it, makes the outcome positive or negative. It is by that potential token that it can be said of life that it is perfect.

Everyday Magic

It might sound somewhat preposterous, but we are all magicians; most of us just don't know it yet. In *The Golden Bough*, Sir James George Frazer elaborates thus on Sympathetic Magic:

> *IF we analyse the principles of thought on which magic is based, they will probably be found to resolve themselves into two: first, that like produces*

like, or that an effect resembles its cause; and, second, that things which have once been in contact with each other continue to act on each other at a distance after the physical contact has been severed. (Page 19b)

From the earlier observation that there is energy in everything (from the stones on the ground to the mere thoughts and intentions of the mind), it can be stated that everything, thoughts or contents of the subconscious mind included, contains energy. Anything you keep thinking about becomes true for you and comes to life because you give it the required energy with your thoughts.

A curious observation of the Japanese researcher, Masuru Emoto in 1994 was the physical effect of words, prayers, music and environment on the crystalline structure of water. His was arguably one of the most amazing experiments ever performed. He hired photographers to take pictures of water that had been exposed to different variables before being frozen to form crystalline structures. He typed out different words, both positive and negative in nature, and taped them to containers full of water. Then came the embarrassing result that water crystals responded to the energy of words! The water stamped with positive words was far more symmetrical and aesthetically pleasing than that stamped with dark, negative phrases.

Knowledge of the fact that positive and negative thinking impact on the surrounding environment, is perhaps common but bringing it out in this very tangible piece of evidence was mind-blowing. If the words and thoughts that come out of us have such an effect on water crystals, then the effects they have on the people, the environment and the events of our lives, are enormous. The important detail, that the average human body comprises 60% water while the brain and the heart are 73% water, makes us ponder about the colossal implications of this finding.

Away from mere water but Similar to Masuru Emoto's was the experiment by Ana Paula Frezatto Martins, a teacher in Curitiba, Brazil. She sealed cooked rice, in two cups and arranged her students in a circle around the two cups of rice. Then she asked them to say bad things to one of the cups – things people might hear in everyday life, like "you are useless", "you are stupid", and "you can't accomplish anything". To the second glass, the teacher asked the kids to say things they would like to hear from everyone. The kids used such expressions as "you are special", "you can accomplish anything", and "you are smart". Days later, the rice in the "love cup" fermented naturally while the rice in the "hate cup" became dark and mouldy. For the record, cooked rice contains between 60% to 68% of water on average. These experiments physically demonstrate the power of magic in the most simplistic way possible as performed unconsciously and every day in streets everywhere and by everybody. Preliminarily, we must watch what we think or say, for we build up or destroy ourselves and others each time.

Magic, as we just saw (not the stage tricks of sleight-handed TV gimmicks), is the process of raising the energy in all things, giving it purpose, and releasing it with the intention to create the desired change or effect.

Magic = energy + purpose

The radiating waves of thought energy about you from another person at any point in time, wherever they might be in the world, can locate you and have an impact on your life. This is pure and simple magic in everyday use evinced in the water and rice experiments above. Consciousness and use of this fact would be to our advantage.

CHAPTER THREE

TOOLS OF BALANCE

Balancing Principles

As far as human beings are concerned, the principles of causality, dynamic equilibrium, balancing forces of nature, their importance and the risks we face in the event of loss of balance of whichever form are a function of the practice of virtue. All virtues are powerful tools of balance in our lives and in nature, but selflessness, gratitude and faith can be considered the embodiment of all other virtues. This is avouched by popular wisdom, but has also been confirmed by empirical evidence from elaborate studies such as the one conducted by Harvard University, which ran for almost 80 years. To enjoy the opulent feeling of accomplishment in old age, selflessness, gratitude and faith are the ingredients. They embody what it takes to manage one's own energy and attitude with wisdom. Practising these virtues is a great influence in the actions and reactions of the individuals to the circumstances they encounter in everyday life.

1. *Selflessness*

While it superficially looks like using up one's substance, selflessness, at root, is the greatest investment a person can ever make of character. It is the art of planting seeds of life, a passive, yet the most gratifying and fruitful of all investments. It is passive because the actor may hardly realize that he or she is planting a seed in the abundant fertility of a person's heart. But it is fulfilling, because it produces an uplifting feeling in the positive touch of others' lives. Its fruitfulness is in fact that, forever, the selfless one will benefit from the returned gratitude of beneficiaries.

> *"We are not born for ourselves alone."* – Marcus Tallius Cicero

My father, whom I have already indicated as one of my private idols, tells of how he was rewarded by his boss for selfless service at his job. As opposed to the employee who sticks to narrow job descriptions, my father went out of his way to help beyond his job description. By that act, he relieved his boss of an otherwise stressful patch in his career. Fast forward, a few years later, when dad embarked on a project to build a house for us – he received considerable assistance from his boss to help him finish the house. Of course, selflessness does not mean giving out everything you have as soon as you get a request to give. What it does mean is that you do *not hold on to that which you truly can let go of, remaining empty of every unspent effort or extra resource to uplift other people in need.* At the very least, selflessness means getting involved in the *sharing economy,* purposively striving to put your idle resources at the service of those in need.

Fox News journalist Danielle Miller in January 2016, told of a baby organ donor who saved the lives of three other children as he died in abusive circumstances:

It all started when a mother left her infant son with the babysitter who she trusted. That little boy ended up abused by the sitter's boyfriend and tragically died, but that tragedy has turned to hope for another family. The infant boy died in 2013 and shortly after, the boy's mother says she didn't think twice about donating her son's organs to save another child.

Today the families gathered with the donor network of Arizona at Phoenix Children's Hospital to meet each other for the first time since the tragedy and life-saving surgery.

"There is another family out there, somewhere, you know, who's feeling something of what I'm feeling, somewhat, and I have the chance to make them not go through what I'm about to go through," said Heather Clark of the decision to donate her son's organs.

Heather Clark made that brave decision to donate her 7-month-old son Lukas' organs after he tragically passed away in June 2013.

"He was just so outgoing, he was just a little ham," said Clark. "If there was a camera in front of him he was either smiling or sticking his tongue out."

Clark says Lukas, her miracle baby for a first-time mother, saved three lives with his organ donation.

One of those lives is that of 4-year-old Jordan Drake, who has spent most of her life inside these same walls of Phoenix Children's Hospital due to a congenital heart defect.

"It's hard to describe... that she would be so selfless to be able to think of another family while she's going through her grief," said Esther Gonzalez.

Lukas now lives on in Jordan. She received his heart, which was the miracle she needed to survive, on June 22, 2013.

"We're family now, we're friends now, our families are families, we've brought our families together," says Gonzalez.

Clark got to listen to her son's heart beating inside Jordan's chest, hearing the gift of life her son gave.

"He was just on the move, rolling, scooting, however he could get there, and that's Jordan, just always going," Clark said.

Both mothers say they'll never forget this day.

Now with this teddy bear that has an audio recording of Lukas's heart, Clark will never have to forget the sound of her son living on....and his life saving sacrifice.

"The only thing I can think of is, I can't save my own son so why not save someone else's child because I can't do anything with him."

Clark tells us she can't say much about the circumstances surrounding her son's death because a criminal investigation is still pending, but she does say it is being investigated as a child abuse case.

As for the two mothers, they say they will find a way to meet up and see each other on a regular basis.

I am under no illusion that everything fits into place and the events find a cordial place in every heart. However, the stark message it gives in rather clumsy tones is that we are definitely not born for ourselves alone.

2. *Gratitude*

Coming from a man with thought clarity as polished as Cicero's, the statement that *"Gratitude is the parent of all virtues"* merits profound consideration. This is more so because the culture of gratitude is much underrated in the modern world, contrasting with empirical evidence which demonstrates its importance in many different ways. Gratitude is a spiritually enriching habit to practise and has been found to be a powerful healing agent:

> *"Gratitude is not only the greatest of virtues, but the parent of all others." –* Marcus Tallius Cicero.

- Professor Robert Emmons, expert in the fields of Personality, Emotion and Religious Psychology, has conducted a lot of studies on gratitude and wellbeing. Repeatedly, he has found that regularly thinking about what you're grateful for can help you feel a lot better, and show up in aspects of your physical appearance.

- Conducted in 2011, another study by psychology professor Nancy Digdon at MacEwan University, Canada, found that subjects who had trouble sleeping because their minds were filled up with different stressful thoughts and worries were able to sleep better by spending 15 minutes to write in a gratitude journal before bed.

- Scientists, generally, have linked gratitude with optimism, and optimism with a stronger immune system. A study by Kiecolt-Glaser et al. (1984) found that participants under stress, but who were more optimistic (who displayed an attitude of gratitude), maintained a higher number of blood cells to protect the immune system. The less optimistic (usually expressed in cynicism or paranoid delusion) participants had less.

Studies after studies reiterate that expressed gratitude exudes such benefits as improving mental strength, looks, psychological health, quality sleep and drastic reduction of aggressiveness and stress levels.

Marcus T. Cicero's quote above makes gratitude the parent of all virtues, and indeed it stands to reason that a genuinely grateful heart can never feel any form of lack. Then, too, other virtues accompany such a grateful heart, besides the fact that persons of such disposition are generally happier.

Gratitude can be viewed as a form of saving. When you receive something from someone, it is only proper to exercise patience in a moment to say a warm and sincere thank you. Doing this sincerely connects you to the giver as you etch your mark on their heart, warming it with more comfort and greater readiness to continue giving. The spur to further give might even be in your own interest or to the interest of someone else who may be favoured because you had shown gratitude in the due time. People who feel and express sincere gratitude greatly ensure themselves against precariousness, a natural spill over from the tendency towards praise or recognition of value characteristic of all of us. Grateful acknowledgement of a gift visibly gives it value. In so giving value to a gift, the receiver raises, so to speak, the value of the giver and of the virtue of giving. This sparks up some form of continuity and the said giver is moved naturally to want to give even more.

By itself, being praised for doing something, motivates the doer to do more of that thing. In the opposite direction, it can be said that a considerable fraction of the miserliness and selfishness in our world today results from the sad habit of people feeling entitled to favours and taking their blessings and advantages for granted. Feeling and expressing gratitude spurs the giver to do more and thus to harness the positive life forces that attract and generate yet more value.

During my boarding days at Baptist High School Buea, it was always a great day which began with this morning devotional song of gratitude:

> *When upon life's billows you are tempest-tossed,*
> *When you are discouraged, thinking all is lost,*
> *Count your many blessings, name them one by one,*
> *And it will surprise you what the Lord has done.*

Science continues to come out with startling findings as it ventures more and more into exploring the benefits of gratitude in the field of Positive Psychology. So far, the benefits are amazing and it is left for us to make the most of what we already know.

3. *Faith*

The principle of faith stretches further than that which is maintained by popular culture; it perhaps stretches slightly wryly from that which is *"Faith is to believe what you do not see; the reward of this faith is to see what you believe."* – Saint Augustine. generally referenced in our various churches. Yet, it tightly intersects with it in the bigger picture. It is this criss-crossing of concepts and practices that make life a vortex of incomprehensibility.

Faith has to be understood here as complete belief or trust in a person or thing, a thing which we fine one way or the other in daily and very common practice: when we go to bed at night, we do so in faith that we will wake up the next morning; when we spend large sums of money to send our children to the best schools, we do so in faith that they will become successful in their various vocations and ambitions. Exercising faith means doing something with the conviction of achieving an expected result. This is against the background that it is possible to do something and not achieve the desired result. In that case, repeating an action or changing the approach increases the chances of achieving the desired results.

Imagine getting home from work and sticking your key into your keyhole, an action which you're so used to performing successfully that you don't even use your conscious mind to do it anymore, and your door doesn't get opened.

You probably would try different turns and positions of the key immediately to increase your chances of making it open. If that fails, you would seek help, perhaps to break the lock and have it replaced with another. Faith, in this example, lies in your knowledge of the fact that regardless of the means you may employ to do so, you are at your house, and you just have to get inside.

Many human projects fail because they are prevented or even perverted by doubt. If you doubt your ability to achieve something, you lower your chances of achieving it simply because you are not motivated enough to put in the necessary push to achieve it. It is that simple. When I decided to start learning to play the piano, I watched a few videos on YouTube and saw how well some professionals played it and recoiled in belief at the prospect of my doing it. I considered that it would be a waste of time for me to venture into trying at all. But ever since I convinced myself that I *can* be like them, I've been putting in an immense amount of energy and time into practising. Today I see myself more likely to hit the professional ranks someday on YouTube. With the faith that I *can* achieve my desire, I am doing what it takes to get there.

Things negative or positive can happen, much depending on the extent to which we believe them to be true. This hard truth has long been exploited in a variety of ways by governments, capitalistic enterprises and even *magicians* over the centuries. Governments have long exploited the power of popular belief through the use of forms of propaganda; corporations have done same using commercials, and *magicians* use conscious energy to realize specific intentions. The word *magician* keeps appearing in italics for the reason that, as broached on earlier, all of us are *magicians*, although most of us do not know it yet, magic being *energy + purpose*. Any outcome you want in life is a purpose, and when you work towards achieving that purpose, you perform magic.

The quality of our lives is essentially a function of the kind of images we entertain in our minds. We witness good and evil things, but when we consciously ruminate on negative images more than on positive ones, when we imagine negative scenarios a lot more than positive ones, we invest thought energy into negative outcomes and give them life, making them manifest to us. The key to using faith to achieve balance in life is surrounding oneself with everything related to that which one wants, and to think mostly about these. Surround yourself therefore with people who are, in one way or the other, related to your dreams and desires, and who carry out the activities that can also somehow lead you closer to these dreams and desires.

I once received an invaluable piece of information from a smart friend of mine, Dr Ebasone. It was a video featuring another smart man in the person of Dr Joseph Murphy, of blessed memory. Dr Murphy was an Irish-American New Thought minister, ordained in Divine Science and Religious Science. In this video, he was explaining what he called the 'Law of Inverse Transformation'. By that law, if you knew exactly how you would feel if you were to realize your dream or objective, if you could replicate that feeling mentally, physically, and psychologically (controlling your state of mind), then the 'Law of Reversibility' would automatically cause your objective to be realized. To put it another way, if a physical fact can produce a psychological state, then, *in reverse*, a psychological state can produce a physical fact. This is a reality already long in circulation amongst psychologists and psychiatrists, and borne out by such realities as psychosomatic illnesses as well as panic disorders and manifestations. Our job then, is to assume and sustain the exact feeling associated with our dreams or goals being fulfilled, until such a time that our dream objectifies itself. To sustain such a feeling, we must live, move, and *be* in that state of belief – the belief that we already are or have that which we desire.

Instead of just making a wish and concentrating on the desired outcome, what you should do is assume the feeling of your dream fulfilled. Thence continue to practice experiencing that feeling until that which you feel is subjected to the balancing law of dynamic equilibrium into becoming your reality. This might be simplistic but it is a cohesive and commonsensical explanation of why and how faith works. It is a thing to be closely and repeatedly studied and internalized.

The fear that keeps us bound to our comfort zones and petrified at the thought of adventure, is the fear of death. While as an unknown reality it terrifies, nothing proves that death itself is neither an exercise of faith, nor a lack of it. There is perhaps nothing to really worry about as far as death is concerned outside the grief of those who will miss our physical presence. The comfort in the book of Isaiah 57:1-2 is that those who walk uprightly enter into peace and find rest as they lie in death.

Faith is an important principle to understand and correctly practice. It gives purpose to life. "Where there is no vision, there is no hope," George Washington said, echoing the biblical "my people perish for lack of knowledge". If evidence is rife on the practicability of faith, why do people not live by it, one might ask. The easy response is that exercising faith is rather tough, and an explanation of why fewer people are happy or successful today. But from the words and works of men and women who, throughout the annals of time, have proven the magical power of faith, such as Jesus Christ and his followers, we imbibe the knowledge and the skill to employ.

Selflessness, gratitude and faith are thus fundamental to sailing the seas of a balanced life into the happy abode of being a well-surrounded old person, comforted by an environment of collective responsibility. It is an environment we should create for ourselves through the quality of our lives. Few things are as painful as regret, and worse is the regret of an aged person wishing s/he had another chance to active life. By diligent application of these principles to daily life, as the saying goes, prevention is better than cure.

4. *Prince and I*: Giving and Gratitude

My encounter with a child hawker, here simply referred to as Prince, made me more aware of the power of giving and of gratitude.

When I met Prince in my university days in Buea, he was a boy of eleven and used to come to sell cooked snails, a delicacy in the region. Whenever I heard the timid voice shout *"Congo meat",* I would immediately jump, open my hostel room door and buy enough of his snail kebab. This was the routine until one day I became inquisitive enough to engage him in a discussion. That is when I learnt that he was eleven years old but was not certain about the pronunciation of his name. We did not venture into the spelling of it because I was visibly embarrassed, my knowledge of illiteracy being cloudy.

Did illiteracy reach such abysmal starkness that a boy of eleven had problems enunciating his own name? But, wonder of wonders, I got to know that he actually held a First School Leaving Certificate. He had completed primary education! He had obtained his certificate two years back. That primary education had ended in the school compound. For he had probably abandoned school and all form of study immediately after schooling. One year was enough to corrupt the fineness of his calligraphy and cause him to misspell and mispronounce his own name. Striking, I was piqued; I wanted to know more about this boy I had thought I knew.

Why did he spend those two years out of school? His mum had gone off to the village to cater for her ageing and ailing father, and his dad had left for the town of Kumba, about one and a half hour's drive from Mutengene, his hometown, to look for a job. Hopefully, he was to send his son back to school in the near future. Prince was left alone, vaguely under the care of his aunt.

In the comfort of a single room apartment, his aunt was not really able to do much for him. But he could be used. So, she cooked snails on regular basis, placed them on his head and had him trek some 15 kilometres to Buea, to sell them.

Physical fitness and resilience? But for an eleven-year-old? That rattled my finer feelings.

By now I had already taken much of Prince's time; he still had a bucket of snail kebab to sell before trekking the tiring way back to Mutengene. Only then could he even think of having a peaceful night-rest at his aunt's house. I let him go, hoping to continue with the discussion next time he came around. I wanted to know more.

So I urged him to knock at my door when next he came hawking in town.

A couple of days later, as I lounged on my couch after my morning classes, I heard a knock at the door. I opened and saw my friend, Kinyang. Beyond him I noticed a transparent bucket full of "congo meat", announcing the long-awaited Prince. He was lost behind my friend's height. The pair had met downstairs, both on their way to my room, but had no idea that they were headed for the same room. Kinyang was surprised that my relationship with the little snail boy had gone beyond buyer-seller banality. He joined me eagerly as we proceeded to pick the pieces of the discussion.

The continuation was even more intriguing, as we were blasted full-faced with the ghastly dismay that walking approximately 15 kilometers from Mutengene to Buea was not enough: Prince was only entitled to one meal. The meal came in the evening, when he returned home from selling. On days when his struggling aunty was dissatisfied with his sales, she brutally beat him up and sent him to bed without a meal. The saving grace was a neighbour who sometimes gave him food without the knowledge of his aunt. If his aunt found out, he would be in serious trouble.

The flow of the story replayed the typical orphan child experience and I was tempted to doubt his it; but honesty radiated from him and clicked with my intuition. In any case, I was not going to start spying on this eleven-year-old to prove that he walked two times 15 kilometres daily or that he was not certain of a meal each day. I took it on trust, first-hand. Could I help him?

On reflection, his story wasn't new. It had a familiar ring to it. Somewhat, it echoed the past of my father. He had also trekked and covered even longer distances, usually to sell food in the market and around our Muaku village. During holiday periods, for a time, my dad walked around very early every morning selling 'puff-puff' prepared by my grandma in her kitchen. She would pile them in a basin big enough to contain what could yield sufficient proceeds to sustain the family. The load in the basin would be covered with cement bags and off my dad would go. My heart ached at the grim familiarity of the hardships people went through to survive. My father was in the distant past and most other such suffering was only of people distant from me. Prince's case rippled as a series of jerks of embarrassing pain.

My friend and I were most surprised at how jovial Prince always looked. His hunger, and having nobody to show him parental love did not take away his glow. A weakening feeling of empathy towards him was inching its way in. Deep down there, I decided that I would lift him up in my own little way.

Going back to school was Prince's dream, what he looked forward to the most and in this we saw his intuitive insightfulness. He strongly believed that someday his daddy would come back for him and send him to school. He just believed. We did not see even the slightest guarantee of that faith but he was convinced beyond any pessimistic dissuasion. He wrenched my heart with that, to me, naïve hope. I feared that a disappointment may be of serious psychological consequence to him. But his faith was touching.

I began meeting him more often and he grew as fond of me as I was of him. He spent a couple of hours to rest in my room each time he came selling, and I made it a habit of giving him a little money at least for his trip back and some feeding. He stopped walking long distances on the highway and began depending less on his aunt for one meal. Six years have gone by and Prince is making progress – he's healthy, schooling, and I'm thrilled that I have become part of his story.

It was such a touching experience when I bought him some school needs for his second year in college. He wasn't selling snails that day. I had asked him to come and collect the things on a day he would not be selling. When he came, I offered him some of the things I was not using anymore and some money with which to buy the rest of his needs, including a new pair of shoes. He was to save some for his transportation allowance. As we interacted that day, I humorously asked: "Prince, what will you give me in exchange for all this? Now I'm broke and I'm sharing what's left of my own allowance with you."

I had barely finished asking my question which was humorous slant intended to ease the atmosphere, when I noticed him fidgeting with a response. He seemed to have either expected the question or had asked himself the same question before. His reply was a repost shot right into my heart: "I will buy you a car, or something a lot bigger than that. If I'm very rich, I will buy you a plane." That was explosive and of course, I'm not expecting a car from Prince, no matter how wealthy he gets in future. The knockout was in his reciprocal intention. I was moved to an extraordinary feeling of fulfilment when I realized the magnitude of his gratitude. I needed nothing more – no car or jet plane. The doping feeling of fulfilment was more than any item could bring about.

Prince is doing well today, though he witnessed his mother die a few years ago. He's in high school and I still communicate with him frequently. I learn a lot from him and study how to uplift him often.

CHAPTER FOUR

VALUE AND SOCIAL INJUSTICE

We each have needs, wants and desires, and face challenges in obtaining them.

In confronting these challenges, we require different facilities in different proportions. A sustained social balance requires every individual to be

"...God owns the earth and all that it contains, the world and all who live in it." Psalms 24:1.

met at their point of need. But who else should satisfy people's needs apart from themselves, families, communities and public service authorities to whom taxes are paid? If there is no other party in the picture, then the fact that many people suffer extreme lack indicates that one party or another has failed to fulfil some of their responsibilities. This chapter elucidates the injustice and the potential danger for society resulting from the inherent imbalance.

The relationship between an individual or family and the society they live in, is like that between an organ and the body it helps sustain. Composed of several trillion cells and some eighty organs, all working together within different systems with the ultimate goal of keeping us alive, the human body is a conjoint of systems carefully structured to keep the entire body healthy and functional. When any one of the organs gets infected, the entire body suffers the effect in different ways. A faulty liver, for example, translates into diarrhoea, nausea and general fatigue. Left unattended, it could even develop into a cancer. Similarly, an unhappy or unproductive component or group within a community or a society, has the potential to cause severe damage to that community. It is of interest to a person to feed healthily to enable the internal organs to work properly and maintain the body healthy. It is for the stability and safety of every community for its component members to be physically, physiologically and psychologically healthy. Their being safe from frustration-induced moral decay would enable them to contribute to the growth and security of their community and not fuel its destruction. Many societies around the world fail in this exercise and the results are always loud enough.

Abraham Maslow's, *hierarchy of needs* projects a practical theory on the progressive nature of innate human values. The natural progression of these human needs must be successively met for all members of any society to be satisfied. Maslow categorized these human needs as follows:

A) Basic needs
- physiological needs (food, water, warmth, rest),
- safety needs (security, safety),

B) Psychological needs
- the need to belong, to love and be loved (friends and intimate relationships),
- self-esteem needs (prestige and feeling of accomplishment)

C) Self-fulfilment needs
- self-actualization needs (achieving one's full potential, creating).

Maslow's theory assumes that we are born vulnerably empty-handed and set on a lifelong mission to participate in the continuous universal process of value creation. So, at birth, we are entirely dependent on values like food and clean water for survival. A comfortable home and adequate security complete our primary needs. Then we grow up and begin forming social ties of collaboration and competition with and amongst each other in order to realize personal and collective ideals. This establishes a much-desired feeling of relevance to society, and then we step up on Maslow's pyramid and seek to achieve our full potential, mostly through various forms of creativity and leadership. Writing and creating works of art, traveling around the world in pursuit of new experiences, knowledge and spiritual enlightenment or, also, aspiring to positions of power on the social ladder…all constitute part of our self-actualization.

Amidst the general desire to move up the *pyramid of wants,* however, a lot of people, as we know, find it extremely difficult to consolidate for themselves the very first level of human needs – the basics of feeding and security. This group of people, hopeless as most of them are, account for a vast majority of the underworld, alongside some of those already situated at the top of the ladder, but who employ evil methods to ascend and stay there. The obvious reason for the inability of those at the bottom to provide for their basic needs is, in greater part, the diverse disparity in the distribution of value around the world. Disparity is evinced at the level of natural resources, education, and technology, as well as power and influence. Even with this uneven distribution of resources, there still exists an opportunity everywhere to create value, albeit a little more challenging. For wherever there is a *human resource*, a thinking mind, there are lingering possibilities of creating value. One of the main obstacles faced especially by those at the bottom of the *pyramid of wants* is the false but crippling belief that all value lies in money. It sets them obsessed with money, causing them to fuel its demand unnecessarily. In the process, they give absolute power to both the money and to those who have much of it.

There is hope of a mass awakening from this fallacious tendency based on new and more sustainable systems of value creation and exchange such as sharing economies, social enterprising and permaculture. These novel trends constitute the main focus in the next section of this book. A deeper understanding of the whole inequality issue and how to overcome it, would require an explication of the concept of value and its proper relationship with money.

Money, Value and Wealth

The subtle difference between being wealthy and being rich escapes the attention of many. A person can get rich overnight and slump back into poverty quickly, but wealth is the durable result of a consistent investment of *real* value. Wealth is much more lasting, more secure, more gratifying and more reliable than an abundant supply of monetary riches. Beyond possessions and monetary accumulation, wealth is a mixture of human connections, knowledge, character, experience, reputation, dignity, respect and other values, often referred to as *virtues*. The wealthy individual commands value from and influences his/her surroundings, without the use of money. They are known and powerful as a result of their personal legacy, more than just for the content of their bank accounts. This kind of value, as expatiated in the next pages, is what has been found to, poignantly, constitute a vast majority of the world's total wealth.

Money does not fall under this category of values since it is merely a componential means to an end, a means to obtain other commodities. It can make a person rich and comfortable but when given greater importance than real values, those which actually constitute wealth, it makes a person extremely vulnerable in the event of loss. What real value does for the persons who holds it in their character and who master it is that, it builds security and affluence around them, making money either abundant in supply or relatively much easier to obtain.

The perennial turmoil of the world comes from many people for centuries making the mistake of actively seeking riches rather than building wealth. The same mistake makes the young people arrogant and disrespectful, makes leaders unaccountable, the clergy dishonest and the old bitter. What these people have in common: they all miss out on the relationship and the difference between money and value, between riches and wealth.

Illustratively, Ebah told us how, in a few months, he ascended to a managerial position in a company which happened to have hired him only as a utility staff. His employer was in the process of setting up a branch for the company in a new location, not too far away from the main branch, and he had the habit of assigning any one of the new employees to go over and help him run errands or oversee the work in progress. The company being small, did not allocate transportation allowances for these errands.

For their part, the staff often went to the boss's office to ask for the fare, all, except Ebah. Perhaps because of this habit aligned with other distinctive practices, Ebah, not surprisingly, was noticed by his boss. His selflessness in not requesting for small money to pay for his taxi drop certainly added positively to his overall dedication in the execution of his job. Ebah had observed that his boss was still struggling to get the company on its feet and did his best to help, giving in every piece of himself in the form of punctuality, availability and humility. His input into the company was soon quite noticeable to anybody with even minimal observational skills. Barely six consistent months into his new job, his boss called Ebah into his office and offered him the task to go and manage the newly set up branch. He was awe-stricken, especially as he knew that there were people in the company who had been working with the boss for much longer.

He had offered real value to his boss and company and now received an opportunity in return, an opportunity to create wealth for himself in the form of the respect and trust of those in his team, the profound consideration of his superiors, and even greater opportunities to create more value. Perhaps Ebah before getting this promotion, did not know that wealth is produced with the heart and not with the hands. It is hoped that his rise was his lesson and that he is creating even more wealth for himself as he serves more and more people wholeheartedly.

We encounter value on a daily basis, but being distracted by the pursuit of money, few of us recognize and treat it as such. We create and exchange value every day in order to survive and thrive as individuals and as communities. That is what being taught good manners as children in our parents' homes, being sent to school to acquire skills for more productivity is all about. We engage or start up various projects, start our own families into which we invest the value we have gathered throughout our lives in order to create wealth for the advancement of our communities.

A person possesses intrinsic value to the measure of the added value to the community. Reducing individual value to communal impact may sound belittling or trite but it is the hard truth. A person who spends more than earned, runs on a deficit. To keep receiving the needed value, a person must also keep generating it for others. It turns out to be less trite, given that value does not require a financial investment at all. We don't pay to be polite, accountable, or available. All we need is to shift from a money mind-set to a value mind-set, to begin cultivating our humanity: it is as simple as smiling more, giving more, forgiving more, being of service and volunteering for good causes.

In February (2018), I was overwhelmed with news of over 1,500 Canadian doctors and medical personnel protesting their own pay raises, asking that the money be redistributed by the system to provide better living conditions for the nurses and some of their patients. These doctors understood the true value of their relationships with their patients, nurse colleagues and society as a whole. They understood that these relationships constitute part of their wealth, and were more important than money. So they could reject a substantial salary increase from the government for the betterment of their relationships with their colleagues and the society.

As a personal development coach, I witness first-hand the fulfilment that comes with focusing on adding real value to the lives of people rather than extracting money from them. It is exhilarating to help people through compelling situations, free of charge, if necessary. Randomly, people contact me for help and in return I enjoy healthy friendly relationships with many of them. While being a paid for service like any other, the real value of what I do on a daily basis cannot be measured in terms of money. Its value lies in the relationships I build with new, well-meaning people.

I look up to Tony Robbins, a seasoned coach who has added value to the lives of millions of people around the world and succeeded over time to build a network of highly productive friendships with many of them. The portfolio of coaching relationships he has today has earned him quite a unique reputation and respect from all over the world. He has contributed to immense successes, the likes of Nelson Mandela, Bill Clinton, Mike Tyson and Serena Williams, just to name a few. Given the scale of his success, Robbins cannot be adequately compensated in financial terms.

I collected notes on the thoughts and experiences of some of my own coaching friends, which I have outlined in the annex at the end of this book. Their testimonies may help emphasize the real value of good relationships in life. Further ahead as you read, you will discover other ways of creating real, rather than monetary value. The take-home principle is that real value is that which produces wealth and peace of mind, while fake or pseudo value may produce money, which sadly is always accompanied by a negative price.

One of my favourite quotes on what differentiates money from value is expressed by the 18th century American social critic, Ezra Pound, who said: "To say that a state cannot pursue its aims because there is no money, is like saying that an engineer cannot build roads because there are no kilometres."

Pound in this statement, draws on the fact that every sovereign government has the power and ability to produce its money. Its central bank controls the amount of money circulating in the economy to ensure that it is proportionate to the sum of the goods and services in that economy, basically to avoid inflation. But then, how can anyone possibly quantify the total amount of value in an economy? Even the World Bank was surprised by their own findings in a recent study, which proved that we cannot truly quantify value in monetary terms. Tarring a road, as per our quote above by Ezra Pound, will be generating real value for an economy through the people whose lives will be made easier by using it. So, if a road should be tarred (thereby adding value to the economy), a government must be free to print as much money as is required to do so (a potential increase in value should imply a potential increase in the money of its Central Bank), so long as tarring that road guarantees a net increase in economic and social value.

Tarring the road is a sample social amenity. Good schools, along with quality study programmes, regular and clean water supply as well as electricity, communication and health facilities are a few more value-adding amenities which a government could thoroughly engage in without regret.

As is the case in many underdeveloped economies today, if the road, for example, is not tarred under the pretext that there is no money, it can clearly be surmised that the said country's economy is under oppressive imperial control. And it can be most emphatically stated that the inherent development problem in "poor countries" is, as it is now widely known, caused by the deception and corruption of imperialism – certainly, never by a lack of money. We do not need to go into the hurtful details of how imperialist states hold down and back the so-called poor countries, but this example gives enough gist on their havoc.

The corrupt rulers of the "developed world" are masters at the trick: they print new money whenever they need more guns and television/cyber "content" to keep the people of the underground-wealthy "third world" countries ignorant and unproductively busy. Thanks to such manipulations, the people are viciously condemned to suffering in belief of lies such as: "their currencies have little value compared to the others'". And so, ignorance kills.

One of the lessons I love to teach the most about wealth, is that it is more of a spiritual than it is a physical asset. Most people spend time working their lives out for money, but those who master the art of creating value, focus more on their character and skill assets than on income.

In a recent discussion with one of my personal development coaching clients, I said "true wealth is not found in money, but in the hearts of people". She became almost annoyingly indifferent in response, probably passing over my statement as just another overhyped inspirational quote. But when I explained a little further and showed her the results of the aforementioned World Bank study on the Wealth of Nations, she was embarrassed to understand how much truth there was in my statement. The verbatim report on the said World Bank study is given below.

This extract of Ronald Bailey's 2007 publication on the online resource *www.reason.com* reports on the findings of the World Bank in a study titled "Where is the Wealth of Nations?" The study exposes the factors responsible for the vast majority of the world's wealth in terms of what have been coined *intangible capital* (i.e., moral and intellectual values). A renowned American libertarian science writer, Ronald Bailey is a contributor to big magazines like Forbes and Reason, lectures in several North and South America universities, and is a writer and editor of books on economics, ecology and biotechnology. He writes:

"Two years ago, the World Bank's environmental economics department set out to assess the relative contributions of various kinds of capital to economic development. Its study, "Where is the Wealth of Nations? Measuring Capital for the 21st Century," began by defining natural capital as the sum of non-renewable resources (including oil, natural gas, coal and mineral resources), cropland, pasture land, forested areas and protected areas. Produced, or built capital is what many of us think of when we think of capital: the sum of machinery, equipment, and structures (including infrastructure) and urban land.

But once the value of all these are added up, the economists found something big was still missing: the vast majority of the world's wealth! If one simply adds up the current value of a country's natural resources and produced, or built capital, there's no way that can account for that country's level of income.

The rest is the result of "intangible" factors—such as the trust among people in a society, an efficient judicial system, clear property rights and effective government. All this intangible capital also boosts the productivity of labour and results in higher total wealth. In fact, the World Bank finds, "Human capital and the value of institutions (as measured by rule of law) constitute the largest share of wealth in virtually all countries."

These findings by the World Bank prove the following statements true:

1. True wealth is not found in money but in the hearts of people.
2. Money is not value. It is a commodity which facilitates the exchange of commodities.
3. Knowledge and morals constitute potential value. And consistently putting them into practical use is what activates the cycle of value and wealth creation.
4. Poverty results not from the absence of money, but from the absence of knowledge and morals or the inability to put them into practice.

Deriving from the above, the question begs to be addressed why knowledgeable and morally upright people remain poor. In response, for starts, let us shift focus from money to value. Evidently these people ignore much potential.

Teach your children and all your family about generating and sharing real value. With this shift in perception, you will build a brand around yourself which will attract real value your way, and you will see opportunities where no one else sees them. If you accept full responsibility for your circumstances, giving a practical objective or mission to your life and removing self-imposed limits, then there is no way you can fail.

Governments of the most developed nations have one thing in common – they give priority to the welfare and education of each of their citizens over everything else. They know that the true value of their economy, as found by the 2006 World Bank study, lies in the hearts and minds of their citizens. Celebrated entrepreneur CEO of Microsoft, Bill Gates, knows this too. On Thursday March 22nd 2018, while addressing the Nigerian Council of State in Abuja, Nigeria, he said, inter alia, about the implementation of economic policy by the government:

> *"...the execution priorities don't fully reflect people's needs, prioritizing physical capital over human capital. To anchor the economy over the long term, investments in infrastructure and competitiveness must go hand in hand with investments in people. People without roads, ports, and factories can't flourish. And roads, ports and factories without skilled workers to build and manage them can't sustain an economy."*

Mr. Gates was quite clear, and hopefully so are we. Thomas L. Friedman in the New York Times (https://www.nytimes.com/2012/3/11/opinion/sunday/friedman-pass-the-books-hold-the-oil.html) in an article entitled "Pass the Books. Hold the Oil" narrates how Taiwan remains one of his favourite countries, despite having no natural resource, being a barren rock and typhoon-laden sea, because *rather than digging the ground and mining whatever comes up, Taiwan has mined its 23 million people, their talents, energy and intelligence....honing [its] people's skills, which turns out to be the most valuable and only truly renewable resource in the world today.*

The author quotes researcher Andreas Schleicher as saying that "education has strong outcomes and high status" in less naturally endowed countries where the public at large

...has understood that the country must live by its knowledge and skills and that these depend on the quality of education...that skills will decide the life chances of the child and nothing else is going to rescue them, so they build whole culture and education system around it.

To prosperous industrialized countries Schleicher says *"the only sustainable way is to grow our way out by giving more people knowledge and skills to compete, collaborate and connect in a way that drives our countries forward."...[since] knowledge and skills have become the global currency of 21st-century economies, but there is no central bank that prints this currency. Everyone has to decide on their own how much they will print.*

It is no doubt great to have mineral and oil resources which can buy jobs, but these resources only weaken the society unless they are used to build schools and a culture of lifelong learning. Thus Thomas L. Friedman who elaborately quotes Andreas Schleicher strongly corroborates the need for skill and culture in economy over physicality.

Social Injustice

In societies where governments marginalize the welfare of its people, poverty and instability are the order of the day. For poor, uneducated people are a high-risk factor to the socio-political and economic stability of any country. They partake in a vicious cycle of evil perpetuated by bad leadership. In the following experience the risk we run when some individuals in society are aggrieved about social injustice, shouts out:

While I walked the streets of Akwa, (a major commercial neighbourhood in the city of Douala, Cameroon), I eavesdropped for a few minutes on the conversation between a pair of *nanga-mbokos,* as the locals call homeless people. One of them was visibly bitter with a worker of a nearby bakery and supermarket (name withheld), near which the *nanga-mbokos* often loitered to beg customers for money and whatever is available for survival. He was angry because a certain lady staff dumped a load of stale pastries and edible residue from their production processes, right before him, into the trash bin.

Apparently, this *nanga-mboko* had asked the lady for whatever foodstuff she had to discard, for him to scavenge on before it gets into the thrash. But for some reason, she did not comply. That was as far as I could listen. From how they sounded as they spoke, I imagined the worst possible reaction, which seemed so feasible: what if these guys, out of frustration and with little to lose, staged an attack on the bakery? Who would lose more?

The feeling of powerlessness that comes with lack can fill a person's heart with enough resentment and bitterness to commit extreme acts of hatred without the slightest remorse.

The sense of ownership inherent in virtually all human beings is a psychological reality even in some animals. How it works is that knowing something or someone intimately starts up a proprietary sense over them. It happens too when you exercise control over someone or something, or spend your time and effort on something. In children, it is observable in that when a child spends some time playing with an object, they resist giving it away.

The sacrificial behaviour of a soldier at the war front to risk their life for an ideal, is primarily motivated by a feeling of ownership of that ideal. That is perhaps why a soldier would feel personally affronted if he saw a civilian in military camouflage. Interpersonal and group conflicts, as well as stiff resistance to change start with the feeling of need to defend some sense of ownership over an item or an ideal.

When the Government Delegate of the town of Yaoundé went around destroying old houses to bring about development, many people were aggrieved. According to some oral accounts, many of them, in rebellion, rejected the compensation which was being offered them by the government for relocation. During a similar event in Douala, one man who had spent many years of effort to put up an apartment building in the Deido neighbourhood, upon being notified that his building was among those to be brought down for purposes of development, went up the building and lay down, asking to be bulldozed all the way down with it.

Attachment is part of human nature, and drawing on a desperate incapacity to comfortably reward one's efforts with a certain degree of material comfort, it can generate extremely violent behaviour.

Back to the need for social equilibrium, it requires that every member of society should have the possibility of ownership; that communities should have access to necessary living facilities, and be given opportunities to ascend Maslow's pyramid of human needs. Failure to assure these dispositions is one of the core causes of extreme inequality and consequent social ills.

The Cost of Injustice

It is perhaps considered virtually normal to see people in positions of authority violating the basic rights of others in exchange for advantages personal to them. In such situations, the potential cost paid by the corrupt individuals and the systems is the negative life force nurtured by the oppressed populations. One does not need a telescopic survey of the distant future to determine that this negative life force affects the economy directly through under-productivity and higher crime rates. You only need to relate the reality to the World Bank study mentioned earlier and its conclusion that the true value of any economy is the combined knowledge and morals of its people. As such, the poorer a people are in terms of these moral and intellectual values, the less performant that economy will be on all fronts.

When you oppress another person, you stake your safety and that of your loved ones. Suffering and unhappiness easily translate into negative emotions, and when negative emotions are intensified through their combination with negative thought, negative actions follow. The formula for magic (***Magic = Energy + Purpose***) and the phrase "thoughts become things" clearly imply that when someone is rightfully angry at you, the emotion creates a permanent condition of precariousness for you.

The more we hurt others, the more vulnerable we are to suffering ourselves. The higher we ride on the heads of others, the more susceptible we are to falling and sustaining injuries. For a while, an oppressed individual may not be aware of being oppressed, but as time passes and if the discomfort increases, they will seek to understand the cause of their suffering, putting the oppressor potentially in trouble.

In Baptist High School Buea, where student hierarchy was very much respected, when younger students got brutally bullied by senior ones, the younger siblings of the bullies in turn suffered from the transferred aggression of the victims. The oppression of people in society registers similar repercussions; it endangers the loved ones of the oppressor by making them targets of vengeful assailants.

Ownership, an Illusion.

Despite being such a strongly held feeling and practice among human beings, the sense of ownership is highly disapproved of by virtually all philosophical doctrines in their spiritual teachings. The French philosopher, Rene Descartes, in his book, *Passions of the Soul* (1649) which he dedicated to Queen Christina of Sweden, wrote: *"nothing really belongs to us other than the free disposition of our voli-*

"The root of suffering is attachment."
—The Buddha

91

tions." And undeniably, despite our claims of ownership over various things, the only thing which truly belongs to us is our willpower, our ability to make choices and the choices we make. In Matt 21:19, Jesus Christ advises a rich young man to sell all his belongings and give the money to the poor, and that doing so would make him perfect with investment in heaven.

This divestment contrasts with social perception where, lack of possessions is synonymous to poverty and vulnerability. It is only to be expected since people use money to do almost everything, indicating the necessity for people to have a minimum supply for self-development and expanded life choices. It is necessary to own assets from which to derive that minimum supply of money to guarantee a sense of security and keep us from descending to or remaining stuck at the base stages of Maslow's pyramid of needs.

The catch is whether there is any point in rushing up a ladder while consciously leaving behind someone who will not hesitate to pull you down by the foot or knock you off the ladder at the least opportunity. The question is whether it is not best to climb up together as a single community unit rather than the individual self-centredness which the social systems in place now uphold.

An individual may truly get rich, but wealth cannot be built individually. It takes a network of like-minded people to build wealth and over time because quick fixes are characterized by short-lived effects. Even the large capitalist corporations we have today were not built on single individuals but on like-minded groups sharing common, agreed-upon values, and are today compensated by huge amounts of money in profit, even though the big question remains: at what cost, in real terms?

We are already conversant with the fact that the quest for material possessions is largely driven by insecurity, which is more or less customary to human beings, one of humanity's primitive survival instincts. Another motivation for the pursuit of possessions is the desire of people to boost their egos in order to feel equal or superior to others in society.

It is supposed that in times long gone people lived in isolated family units, exposed to the dangers of the wilds. Human life had little purpose as men and women lived to farm, hunt, reproduce and die. There was no need for any ambition or competition beyond striving to survive, given that community life was almost inexistent. Things are different today. We subsist in densely populated metropoles and compete amongst ourselves for status and possession, self-gratification and social validation. We compete to boost our egos far more than we collaborate for collective interests and the progress of our communities. We miss out on the fact that our survival as communities depend on the survival of each individual member of these communities and vice versa.

When one organ of the body is infected, the entire body is sick, to paraphrase the Apostle Paul. Thinking you are secure, when your neighbour is not, is a false perspective to entertain. A sick and unhappy family member produces a sick family, unless that family deliberately disconnects itself completely from the sick member, which itself makes the family dysfunctional relative to the disconnected part. It is true that some members of our community are insatiable and that it is nobody's job to satisfy anybody at all. We, however, have a duty to stay empty of unspent effort and use such effort to generate value and promote satisfaction in any way that we can, thereby contributing to the overall health of our communities.

The popularity of self-centredness in today's world is only the reflection of our current worldview, which is pigeonholed in fear and negativity, a mentality enforced by the mainstream media. People have learned unconsciously to live in constant fear of a variety of things, including disasters, burglaries, hunger, shame and self-doubt.

In several cultures in the past, especially in Africa, sharing and collective responsibility were so deeply entrenched in society that they constituted the norm. Similar modes of living are still practised in some places today.

A little way back, in my father's childhood in our village, for example, the boys traditionally met in groups on certain mornings. They then moved around the village, working on the farms of their parents or those of whoever needed help along their way. They did not each wake up in the morning and go to their various parcels of land. Rather, they came together and took on one farm at a time, finishing their work on each farm in record time and moving to the next, quickly lending a helping hand to every farmer they came across on their way. When they returned to their various homes at the end of the day, they cleaned themselves up and re-joined each other in one house for dinner as a commune. The notion of collectivism was prized then.

Today, people are more individualist by default, thanks to a worldview of fear and self-centredness canalized by mainstream media. It can be changed.

The massive collective that we really are as one race is separated into various smaller, easily controllable groups by illusory labels such as skin colour, religious beliefs, and political leanings. These labels have consistently shifted our perceptions from unity to that of egotism. We can identify ourselves in this illusion and generate abundance in our lives as a collective, deciding to wake up from it and for good.

The Great Misconception

The following statistics on the results of socioeconomic inequalities around the world are strong indicators of the repercussions of inequity:

Mexico

In 2015, statistical reports found that 43% of Mexico's wealth was held by 0.002% of the country's population. During the same period, 13 of the 20 deadliest cities in the world were found in Mexico.

China

An estimated 90,000 riots occur every year in China, and the bulk of these take place at the 'border' between urban and rural areas, where poor families can witness first-hand, the vast disparity between the rich and themselves.

Sierra Leone 1991

1991 marked the start of a brutal civil war in Sierra Leone, which broke out when the country was facing a steep economic downturn with a per capita Gross National Income of $180 in the same year, earning it a position on the list of the world's poorest countries.

Cote d'Ivoire 2000

Cote d'Ivoire witnessed its first post-independence civil war in the year 2000. Its per capita Gross National Income declined steadily from $1,120 in 1980 to $650 in 2000 which moved thousands of average income earners from their average situations into abject poverty.

Baltimore 2015

According to a February 2015 report from the Justice Policy Institute on the high poverty levels in Baltimore, 51.8% of the working-age residents of Baltimore were unemployed between 2008 and 2012. The 2009-2013 U.S. Census report found that 23.8% of the population live below the poverty line, and according to City-Data, 29.4% of children were living below the poverty line in 2009. The violent 2015 protests which were triggered by the death of Freddie Gray, were not a mere coincidence.

Ferguson 2014

In addition to the highly significant rates of race-based inequality in the area, the poor population of Ferguson, Missouri, doubled between 2010-2012, with 21% of its population living below the Federal poverty line. That translates to 1 in every 4 people living in severe poverty. Within the same timeframe, almost all neighbourhoods in the area had poverty rates at or above the 20% threshold at which the negative effects of concentrated poverty begin to emerge. With such statistics, the violent and deadly protests which were immediately triggered by the fatal shooting of Michael Brown by a police officer, come as no surprise.

DR Congo 1998 - Present

Following the poverty/violence trends in richer countries, one would wonder what to expect from the "poorest" nation in the world, despite its wealth of natural resources, the Democratic Republic of the Congo. Due to its lack of a strong central government, the DR Congo has been subject to decades of conflict over basic and economic resources. The waves of greed and corruption at the top led to extreme poverty at the base population, in turn leading to the rise of several violent groups in the region, many of which took advantage of the Tutsi invasion of the DR Congo before the 1996 First Congo War. Inequality-related violence has thrived in DR Congo till present day.

Iran 2017

On December 28th, 2017, a series of violent protests occurred throughout Iran as a result of economic hardship. The immediate cause of the protests, which continued into 2018, was an increase in food prices which led hundreds of poor families far below the poverty line.

Tunisia, Dec 2010 – Jan 2011

The office of longtime Tunisian President Zine El Abidine Ben Ali came to an end in January 2011 after an intense wave of violent public demonstrations against extreme poverty, social inequality and political repression. The immediate cause of these protests which spread to almost all Arab countries as well as others like the United States, Gabon, Albania etc., was the self-immolation of 26-year-old Mohamed Bouazizi in front of the provincial police headquarters. Bouazizi, a hawker, and sole income earner of his family, set himself on fire as a result of his frustration following the confiscation of his merchandise by a police officer, Faida Hamdi.

France, 1789-1799

The social and financial inequality which characterized France in the latter part of the 18th century was among the main causes of the historic French Revolution of 1789-1799. The abusive extravagance of Queen Marie-Antoinette and the debt-ridden state of the French economy under the rule of her husband, King Louis XVI, were enough to bring multitudes of peasants to the streets in violent protest.

The list is inexhaustible, but strongly points to the correlation between extreme poverty and violence. With this background in mind, one cannot miss the deep truth in the words of the teacher, Henry W. Longfellow: "If we could read the secret history of our enemies, we should find in each man's life sorrow and suffering enough to disarm all hostility." These statistical facts indicate that what lies ahead in terms of world peace is nothing flattering. The good news is that checks will check it, ours being a world of natural balances, where the crises of inequality are soon balanced by forces of nature, unless we pre-emptively resort to resolving the said crises by ourselves.

The sub-titular *great misconception* describes a wave of ignorance that has taken most of the world hostage; value in our world today has been entrusted into money and possessions at the expense of humanity and the development of spiritual potential. Does anybody deserve to struggle for a meal while others have more than they can ever consume?

By virtue of our humanity and as a conscious and creative collective, we each possess intrinsic value. But we live in communities where it is a big challenge for some people to have a single meal in a day. At the same time as is, NASA and other high budget fancy agencies spend billions of dollars every year to do rarefied researches, like finding life and water on Mars, while potable water remains a huge challenge in many parts of the world, especially in Africa.

Where are the values of humankind? If a farmer makes a harvest, sells his produce and keeps the rest to waste because nobody would pay for them, then he has transferred his perception of value to the representative piece of paper that money really is. Such an action constitutes *the great misconception*. It constitutes the collective mistake made in different ways by actors in our globalized capitalist economic system, and one reason for the system's precarious and extreme vulnerability.

PART TWO

CHAPTER FIVE

A NEW ORDER

Neuroscientific research has discovered mirror neurons in the brain, which enable people to feel what others feel. The said mirror neurons are the mechanism responsible for empathy, for compassion towards oneself, and for self-love. When you feel like yawning just after seeing someone else yawn, your mirror neurons are responsible for that. They reflect the same feeling and arouse it in you. These premises imply that the mirror neural system is influential in determining people's relationship with themselves, and their levels of mental health.

When you display social responsibility towards your environment, you enhance your empathic abilities and strengthen your mirror neural system, thus developing a better mental health state for yourself. This brain science finding supports the long held saying that "giving is receiving". Contrary to popular views that selflessness is synonymous to self-sacrifice, neuroscientific findings, hold that altruism benefits the giving party much more than we could have imagined in the past. When we act in a negative and insensitive manner, our mirror neurons are weakened and our empathic abilities drop. With that, our self-esteem and overall mental health also decrease.

Yet the benefits of altruistic behaviour are many. From the above premises and from what you will read in the rest of this book, you can further your research to uncover these in people. It is valuable knowledge that is largely unexploited, which is perhaps why a lot of people fail to realize that they harm themselves when they harm or ignore others.

It is wrong to hold the impression that everything is wrong with the world and that it is almost impossible to fix. No, the world does look that horrible. What is projected and worth sticking to is that love and light will always conquer hatred and darkness and that justice will always prevail over injustice, no matter how long it takes.

Chapter one explained that, we each have a part to play in the grand scheme of things, based on our worldviews or belief systems; that we possess the power to influence and enact great changes in the world simply by changing our own attitudes and our beliefs, transmitting our good practices to our families and neighbours. Concentrating our attention on positive media will enable our mirror neurons to trigger us to reflect positive actions. A ripple effect surely to ensue is the wave of change which will sweep over the earth and break the evil standards to which humanity has so far been accustomed.

There are simple socio-environmental and economic practices which, on a large scale, have the potential to change things in this manner. Only, we must make these practices trendy by carrying them out and making them a culture within our circles. Mainstream media being under the control of power-thirsty oligarchs, is mostly focused on distributing what pushes forward the agenda of its owners instead of educating populations on practices that empower them.

Some of these practices and how they can bring about a revolution if carried out on a large scale are elaborated below. They include the *Sharing* and *Gift Economies*,

Green Economy, Creating Shared Value, Collective Social Responsibility and Permaculture.

What if people were to share everything from their deepest pain to their greatest pleasures in a society governed by high moral standards, a high degree of transparency, with resources sustainably used? In such a set-up nothing would be wasted, but put up for sale to someone else to use, or it is put up for rent, or even gifted to the poorer populations, if no one would pay for it.

This is not utopian, for a combination of some of these values is already upheld and practiced in different forms and in different places around the world and known as *Sharing Economy*. Although it may be hard to scientifically evaluate the extent, popular observation supports that sharing Economy is contributing substantially to ecological balance. If businesses could integrate this practice through measures such as offering up goods approaching expiry to poor and needy persons for free or in exchange for unskilled services which they would otherwise pay wages for, they would be *creating shared value*.

Here then is the challenge of modern business, one which through the enterprise of this book we are undertaking to disseminate. It is hoped that businesses will be helped to integrate the concept of *creating shared value* into the running of their enterprises. It costs little and takes hardly any extra effort, despite its potential to generate wealth in the long run and increase the size of a company, through building a new and improved relationship between the company and its market.

Stronger Human Relationships

Building and maintaining relationships is a fundamental aspect of human life, already indicated as one of the core concepts explored here. Relationships cut across all human endeavours from family life through to business and recreation. We are born with relationships and we create new ones in due course, striving to exploit and maintain them until we die.

As a social species, we are compelled to maintain relationships for a wide variety of reasons, all revolving around self-interest. Human beings are naturally self-centred, and all their relationships are really based on this natural tendency. We strive to satisfy our personal desires or the desires of loved ones. In this way, the wry humour is that altruism itself gets motivated by selfish interests. Even when the altruistic act goes to those less close to the altruist, the fact remains that the post-altruistic good feeling propels altruism, and that altruism is self-satisfying. True, altruism is an urge to give happiness to others, but if altruists do not do so, they do not feel good about themselves.

Illustratively, if your sibling falls ill and needs a kidney transplant, and you are the only available donor, you would donate yours because you love your sibling and still need him/her around. You could also donate yours because you want to avoid being considered responsible for his/her possible death. Your motivation revolves on your interest, one more distant than the other. It is not flattering to be considered as one of the "selfish species", but there is more to it than that.

Selfishness is excessive preoccupation with one's interests, without regard for the interests of others. But what can the self really *possess* which did not come from without? We are born naked and empty-handed into the world, where we meet pre-established relationships that provide us with the things we need to survive on. We grow up creating new relationships by which to obtain what we desire in life, including wealth, happiness, knowledge and experiences. The question is how to get the desired value out of relationships without causing harm to others or leaving them lacking. The golden rule is also a rule of thumb – *giving*. Value is bound up with giving.

Complementarity is the quality of two things mutually filling out or completing each other. Both things give themselves to each other in order to be complete. It is through the simple or complex process of giving in relationships that dynamic equilibrium is maintained. The marriage relationship depends on complementarity (giving from both ends) unto dynamic equilibrium. The following extract of a speech by Pope Francis I at a colloquium in the Vatican Synod Hall in November 2014 explains how this concept evolves in the marital union:

> *When we speak of complementarity between man and woman in this context, let us not confuse that term with the simplistic idea that all the roles and relations of the two sexes are fixed in a single, static pattern. Complementarity will take many forms as each man and woman brings his or her distinctive contributions to their marriage and to the formation of their children — his or her personal richness, personal charisma. Complementarity becomes a great wealth. It is not just a good thing but it is also beautiful.*

Complementarity creates wealth not only in marriage but in all human relationships. Countless times the argument is heard about man versus woman, some for equality, others for patriarchy and other constructs, backed by religion, history, philosophy, biology, etc. For the most part, these arguments are entertained with nothing serious in mind. Seriously, men and women are different in ways and for reasons that go deeper than individual and even scientific understanding. In the debate of the sexes on complementarity and dynamic equilibrium the finale is that *we need each other.*

The bigger picture on creationist and evolutionist fronts, remain that the sexes complement or complete each other for the human race to perpetuate itself. In this complementarity, all parties focus on giving, and in the process, they receive in perpetuity. Thus, in a classic family construct, the husband strives to give physical protection and material comfort to his woman; the woman gives her attentive care and respect to her man who gives reproductive cells to her and she brings forth children into their home; the children bring joy to their parents; the parents give food, clothing and education to the children; the children grow up to give more value to the society, etc., and the cycle continues.

A consistency noticed is that at no point in the relationship does anybody have any *responsibility* to receive. Our responsibility is to give, and focus only on giving. In the process, all parties keep receiving.

Beyond human relationships, we have relationships with things. These, too, respect the central value of giving. We give our time and attention to the projects we undertake and the causes we defend. We give out our money into investment opportunities, advice friends and family, complement deserving people, etc. Whether "rich" or "poor", all we are called upon to do in a world of dynamic equilibrium is *give*. Giving is attested to in most religious groups as important and rewarding.

- *"One gives freely yet grows all the richer; another withholds what he should give, and only suffers want. Whoever brings blessing will be enriched, and one who waters will himself be watered."* – (Proverbs 11: 24-25)

- *Give, and it will be given to you... for the measure you give will be the measure you get back.* (Luke 6: 38)

- *Those who act kindly in this world will have kindness.* (Islam, Qur'an 39:10)

- *"If beings knew, as I know, the fruit of sharing gifts, they would not enjoy their use without sharing them, nor would the taint of stinginess obsess the heart and stay there. Even if it were their last bit, their last morsel of food, they would not enjoy its use without sharing it, if there were anyone to receive it."* (Buddhism. *Itivuttaka* 18)

- *"The Buddha said, 'When you see someone practicing the Way of giving, aid him joyously, and you will obtain vast and great blessings.' A shramana asked: 'Is there an end to those blessings?' The Buddha said, 'Consider the flame of a single lamp. Though a hundred thousand people come and light their own lamps from it so that they can cook their food and ward off*

Contrasting these religious counsels is the capitalistic tendency to value profits over and above building and maintaining healthy relationships. By all measures, this is one of the root causes of the poverty and inequality constructs. By way of reservation, this is no accusation of diligent business people of total responsibility for poverty. For the "poor" themselves, in their lack of knowledge and rigid belief systems, are usually erroneously envious and attached to the wrong things. They focus on receiving instead of giving. They stay perpetually in want and in the belief that they cannot give, claiming the excuse that they are poor. The 'poor' miss out on the entire point of prosperity throughout their lives. But sustained poverty devolves on the principle of dynamic equilibrium: not giving and receiving gratitude, the poor do not receive and so lock themselves up in a cycle of perpetual want. They are gagged by the great misconception, a misconception which roots virtually all man-made societal suffering today.

Poverty would be diminished greatly if the poor came together in support groups or *sharing economies*. Rather than begging from the rich, the poor should share with each other the little they may have – resources, knowledge and skills – and work towards their collective progress. It will come to light in that process, that a lack of money is not the same thing as poverty, and that poverty is rather a lack of knowledge and people relationships.

The Power of Human Networks

A network of good friends is an asset which not everybody can boast of since many people are hindered from building new friendships by past issues of trust with friendships. This is the result of yet another misconception – that of expecting rather than offering. Friendship is about mutual giving and true friendships are established around giving. One who receives will want to give in return. If they don't, the relationship soon dies naturally, which of course, should not disturb the giving party in any way, unless they made the mistake of expecting instead of focusing on their role of giving.

"Personal relationships are always the key to good business. You can buy networking; you can't buy friendships."
– Lindsay Fox

The law of reciprocity embedded in the human DNA is that when people receive, they feel compelled to give. It is on this principle that the gift economy, as elaborated later, runs and thrives. When giving is practised deliberately in an organized group or network such as in a gift economy, it becomes a force which tremendously benefits its members in different ways and areas of their lives. Poor and rich people can be effective members of the same network, if they all focus solely on giving – services, advice, errands, useful information, unused items, etc.

One of the inventors of Ethernet technology, Robert Metcalfe, came up with a simple formula to measure the value of telecommunications networks. By the judgment of many, the formula can be applied to measure the value of human networks. His derivation was as follows:

value of network = number of users^2

Robert Metcalfe's law has however been criticized by other schools of thought for various reasons, in favour of new formulas. American Electrical Engineer, Nathan Black, has derived the following formula as the value of networks:

$$Total\ network\ value = n^2 \sum_{n=0}^{total\ n} value\,(n)_{received}$$

Several other researchers have come up with proposals about the power of networks. However different and complicated their formulas are, all agree on the great value found in networks. Some even consider the growth in value per added member to the network to be as exponential as Robert Metcalfe had determined.

Labour unions, governments, all businesses and organized religions are basically built on the power of networks. Think of yourself as a brand and think of everybody else as a potential member in your consumers' network, people who consume the value you create. All the people you help in one way or another will become part of your network.

The gift economy, as earlier described, is a mode of life practised by different groups around the world, where valuables are not traded or sold, but rather given out without an explicit agreement for immediate or future rewards. This way of life is based on the merging of the principle of reciprocity and the known power of networks. It produces a positively overwhelming experience of life, and the best way to experience this is to create your own network, i.e., to bring people together in a giving continuum, starting with your trusted friends and family. Start giving favours to one another and to other people. Grow this network over time by adding more people and more families and see what you will get out of it.

Group action is exponential, always bearing far greater results than individual action. The amazing part is that your experience of life will be greatly enhanced from within such a community as you may learn a lot and give greater purpose to your life; you may become happier, thereby attracting more good things your way. Go ahead and give it a try. You have nothing to lose.

Temperament and Relationships

Building strong relationships with people has a lot to do with temperament. This paragraph is likely to trigger reality check and a self-analysis regarding personal relationships. Your temperament, your

A man's happiness or unhappiness depends as much on his temperament as on his destiny. –
Francois de La Rochefoucauld

overall psychological nature, your character and psychology identify four standard temperaments:

- **Sanguine** – *enthusiastic, active, and social.*
- **Choleric** – *short-tempered, fast, or irritable.*
- **Melancholic** – *analytical, wise, and quiet.*
- And **Phlegmatic** – *relaxed and peaceful*

These demarcations, however, contain grey areas, as an individual may show signs from different temperament groups. From several scientific studies, there have been focus on the relationship between temperament and overall performance at various tasks. A 2017 study by Dr Kehdinga George Fomunyam and Dr Thoko Mnisi on temperament and students' performance in the University of KwaZulu Natal, South Africa found that "sanguine students obtained better scores in formative assessment than phlegmatic and melancholic students but came second to choleric participants. This is primarily because although like cholerics, sanguines are extroverted in nature, they tend not to follow through on tasks" (Steiner, 2008).

It may be useful to know which group you belong to, but it is more important to be conscious of your attitude at all times and monitor aspects that are detrimental to your relationships. You can then employ sustained effort to change them.

Our demeanour influences how people relate to us. A welcoming and pleasant attitude at all times keeps our doors open to receive whatever the world may have in store for us. The happiest people in life are usually not any better off than the sad ones, except for their happy temperaments, their natural joyful states.

If you are a Christian, chances are you might have read the Apostle Paul's letter to the Philippians. It is filled with joy, in spite of the fact that he was imprisoned in a Roman jail at the time he wrote the letter. His happiness did not depend on external circumstances; it came from within. Somehow, he had attained a joyful state of being, and had cultivated a vast network of good, healthy relationships.

A joyful temperament is the unavoidable result of the habits of gratitude and giving. It has the potential to completely alter your experience of life beyond imagination. Every interaction you make is an opportunity to plant a seed of goodness in your heart and in that of those you interact with. It is the opportunity to open a door through which you may need to pass in future.

We keep the memory of other people based on how we were treated by them. Most of the time it is unconscious, but the human spirit feels and understands the energy directed to it by other spirits and keeps records instinctively in the subconscious mind. Some casual interactions are easily judged as unimportant, but may surprisingly be profound. In this respect, John Maxwell's, *Everyone Communicates, Few Connect* is a book to read as it throws light on the power of human interaction and how to make a positive impact at the slightest opportunity to interact with someone. Having acquired people skills as those preached in the book by John Maxwell, creating and integrating help networks such as a *sharing economy* would be made a lot easier for an otherwise difficult personality.

The Sharing Economy

The expression *Sharing Economy* is still subject to academic analysis and generates some controversies about its standard definition. It is used freely in this book to refer to a revolutionary economic model of collaborative consumption, in which people exchange goods and services directly or indirectly. The model highlights necessity, trust, an effort to minimize waste of useful resources and the will to help others in need. It includes barter, representing an effective antidote to the misdoings of pure and often ruthless capitalism. Its advantages include increased sense of security and trust in a community, amplified number of money-making opportunities and hence easier access to capital for the less privileged.

A homeowner letting out a free room of their house to a pair of tourists for the weekend is an example of the sharing economy in practice. It has recently been popularized by *Airbnb*, an online company which links homeowners around the world to people seeking temporary lodging facilities. Other examples of companies providing amazing services in the *Sharing Economy* are *NeighbourGoods*, *Poshmark*, *Uber*, *RelayRides*, *Zaarly*, *Fon and TaskRabbit*. Reading about these can be an amazing discovery on the available and how they make life simpler and more fulfilling, especially for the less privileged.

Away from the internet, the *Sharing Economy* in different ways has always been, and is still practised physically in many African villages. We have already referred to the group relay work of youths in the village where my father would spend his boyhood holidays. What still goes on is a sustainable clothing policy in which older siblings' clothes are handed down to younger siblings and other younger children in the community. The growing ones getting bigger, inherit the clothes of older ones and the process is repeated, until the clothes get totally worn out and unusable. This helps the various families to save clothing money and avoid waste of useful resources. The policy also applied to and is still practised with school books, stationery and other commodities.

Sharing communities open up available resources and opportunities for use by others who may in return give resources or services to reduce waste and create better societies. The process debunks the illusion of poverty, for, again, poverty does not mean or imply the absence of money, but rather the absence of shared values.

Creating Shared Value

The world as our habitat is our collective responsibility to protect, if it must continue sustaining our life on it. Now, we cannot look after our environment without looking after each other as fellow inhabitants. We are all part of an interdependent ecosystem. We depend on each other and the environment, and our environment depends on us to a great extent. There is no way out of this web.

The concept of Shared Value is an ecological haven which cannot be overemphasized, since our survival and wellbeing as a species depend on that of the environment. The capitalization of social problems through the use of economic models to provide lasting solutions, is shared value. The objective of every business venture should be to solve a *real* social problem, to a true social need. As in the World Bank's 2006 study, referred to in Chapter three above, global economy is driven by human values, not by money. If this were widely known, the inequality problem itself would, as in the case of proper diagnosis, be already half cured or even not exist at all.

Business aside, Creating Shared Value is an aspect of everyday life. Providing solutions to each other's problems in a community is an act of Creating Shared Value. I currently run a restaurant and natural juice bar, producing loads of organic waste on a daily basis, the kind of things pigs feed on. One of my team members had the genius idea to bring in one of her neighbours, a rather aged man, who rears pigs in his backyard for a living. Having the necessary facilities to transport our waste to his home, he provided us with an easy solution to our waste disposal problem at zero cost, while at the same time spending less effort and no money to provide his pigs with a much healthier diet – we both created and Shared Value for ourselves, and also for the community through the disposal of loads of otherwise unpleasant waste, as well as odour and visual pollution.

Creating Shared Value can hardly be discussed without mention of Michael E. Porter, an economist at Harvard Business School, and Mark R. Kramer, CEO of American business consulting firm, FSG. Both are renowned proponents of the Shared Value concept, holding that *a shared value approach to business must intimately connect the company's success to social and environmental progress.* This requires consideration of the social and environmental consequences in all activities before we undertake them. Business or any other activity would only be given a pass if proven to have an overall positive impact on society.

Beyond just practising corporate social responsibility, responsible companies in modern times must have Shared Value incorporated into their corporate fabric, or at the very least, have an organ which caters exclusively for the company's objectives being tailored to social responsibility and the creation of Shared Value. Such an organ would ensure that the company's executive strategy respects set provisions to this effect. This holistic approach to business, amongst myriad advantages, emphasizes the social nature of humanity by strengthening cohesion and hence stability in any given society, besides enforcing effective altruistic thinking among its members.

Effective Altruistic Thinking

Altruism is understood to be selfless concern for others. To be effective, altruism should mean helping others in the most efficient way possible. Offering fish to a hungry fellow is an altruistic act, but an effective altruistic act would be teaching them how to catch fish,

"Charity is not giving people what you want to give, it is giving people what they need to get." Terry Pratchett,

addressing their problem more efficiently and sustainably. The media-enforced impression that the world is full of negativity belies the fact that a lot of good is actually going on. Only, it is not the focus of mainstream media. However, a growing number of people are trying to help raise that awareness as much as possible. In the endeavours to be of help, one big challenge is identifying the right strategies to that effect. The perennial question every aspiring social entrepreneur asks is: *"How best can I be of help?"*

Many organizations specialize in carrying out elaborate studies to detect the best causes to support so as to guide the efforts of altruists towards giving charity in an effective manner. They investigate the most effective charity organizations to which donors may provide support in order for their donations to reach the final consumer and have greater impact. Effective Altruism Funds (app.effectivealtruism.org) is one such organizations.

As an individual, developing an effective altruistic way of thinking means thinking like a social entrepreneur, or a Shared Value creator, that is, looking for the best possible way to solve a problem and focusing more on the social and spiritual benefits rather than just the financial. I saved a beautiful article from years ago with the purpose of sharing it in a book someday. It seems relevant right here. It is titled "The Economics of Compassion" by C. Eugene Steuerle, who is introduced as an American economist, a Richard B. Fisher chair and Institute Fellow at the Urban Institute in Washington, DC. He is a columnist under the title "The Government We Deserve" and his January 5th, 2012 number, reads:

In a world of 24-hour news cycles, nonstop political campaigns, and persistent public policy failures, it's easy to lose perspective. But a new day or a new year offers new hope, so let's pause to ask who and what makes this world a better place.

Economists see great value in people trading their services and goods. When two parties make free exchanges, both believe they will gain from the action. So, when such exchanges are blocked by monopolists, dictators, or bad laws, collective welfare is reduced.

But isn't it a bit of a stretch to argue that the good life is obtained exclusively or even mainly by market trade or proper government regulation and taxation of such mar-

kets? It's not so much that self-seeking people sometimes don't play the game fairly and might cheat, lie, steal, create Ponzi schemes, sell inferior products, collude, or market falsely. It's that they don't fully realize their potential for doing good.

Here, almost all religions are united in promoting one virtue that makes us more fully alive and the world a better place: compassion. The golden rule expounded by everyone from Confucius to Buddha to Jesus to Hillel bids us to treat others as we would be treated.

I would add a corollary to that rule of old, one that attempts to prove in economic terms that self-seeking is not enough:

The golden rule needs to be seen as more than a matter of belief. The moral compulsion to follow it is driven by our species' fundamental, even biological, drive to survive and regenerate and, uniquely, to build and improve. If one could quantify this moral imperative, it's that if you do good for me and I do good for you, we will multiply the combined good achievable when we try to do good only for ourselves.

We have the power to help others far more than ourselves.

The evidence is obvious, once you reflect on it. What's the most important event of my life or yours? Isn't it that we were born? What influence did each of us have on that event? Absolutely none. Fundamentally, we don't deserve life because of our own actions; it is a pure gift. Yet, we can and do participate in the birth of other people, ideas and memories, events and institutions all of which have lives of their own. Isn't our power to participate in the miracle of birthing greater for others than for ourselves?

Or take the other end of the life cycle. How much domain do we have over death? Perhaps we can delay or speed up our own day of destiny, but that's about the extent of our control over our situation. Even then, each of us has but one life. But when it comes to others, we have much more power, and much more than our ancestors did. Recent wars, terrors, and acts of violence make it clear that almost any of us can easily kill many people and destroy many lives. But the flip side of recognizing this power to do evil is also worthy of note. We have an equal, perhaps greater, power to do immense good. We touch on thousands of people over the course of our lives. And many of us lucky enough to live in this time and place have the wherewithal needed to save or improve the lives of many people.

Think now about the countless problems that we let get to us day after day. For most of us, hardly a day goes by when we do not want someone else to extend to us some love, job, promotion, access, favour, or simple recognition or, in the case of government, to enact the policies that we favour. But waiting for others to do something for us can be debilitating, occupying time better spent else-

where. And when we become too absorbed in what we want from others, we can't see the consequences of our actions and inactions or really hear others and respond to their needs.

While we can't easily change what others are inclined to do for us, we can change our own behaviour toward them. Anyone who has ever raised children quickly learns how little control we have over them, compared to ourselves.

At this time of the year, therefore, my thoughts and thanks go out more than ever to all of you who partake in the birthing and rebirthing of a better world.

Eugene Steuerle's wisdom and truth ricochets on

- The over-regulation of trade by government that reduces collective welfare.
- Our possessing much more potential to help others than we do to help ourselves.
- It being much more profitable to spend our time giving than to spend it merely expecting from others.
- It being our responsibility to give to others.
- And that life is only a gift, and our actions should reflect gratitude thereof.

The Gift Economy

A system of value transfer, an economy where goods are not traded, but given freely, with no explicit agreement for an immediate or future reward is what is here referred to as the gift economy. Its peculiarity is that it relies on shame and honour. A receiver feels obliged to provide value of some form to the giver at a later date to preserve their honour, or face shame if they fail to do so. Some scholars argue that this practice is based on self-interest, but as earlier specified and from every indication, every human endeavour is based on self-interest of some form. Gifting must be seen as a healthy and sustainable practice for, instead of keeping resources idle and wasting, they are circulated and put to use to benefit those who might need them. Gift economies involve two or more people forming an organized group in which favours are granted and gifts offered for the greater good of the collective.

Permaculture

Largely underrated, permaculture is one discipline which holds the key to sustainability in today's anthropocentric world. The term was coined by David Holmgren and Bill Mollison in 1978 from *permanent agriculture* and *permanent culture,* to basically refer to the conscious and holistic replication of natural closed systems in the human setting, in order to minimize waste and help preserve nature. It cuts across several aspects of human life, including economics, waste management, hydrology, technology, agriculture, natural building and community development, amongst others. As an underlying philosophy, permaculture opts to work with nature, instead of against it, to follow nature's observable patterns and principles so as to integrate them in the ecosystems and everyday life.

A standard example of a home designed following the permaculture principles would look something like this:

It is situated along a gentle slope, roofed with solar energy panels bordered by water collecting pipes. These pipes channel rain water into a suspending barrel which connects to an irrigation system that uses gravity to water the backyard garden in the dry season. A few meters out the backdoor, there is a wide trough dug out for the formation of compost. This trough has about three different layers in the form of steps, and organic waste is dumped into the first layer up, and gradually pushed down with the help of gravity as the first layer fills up, eventually becoming fully developed compost at the third layer which is used to cultivate the vegetable garden in the backyard.

On a large scale, permaculture has tremendous impacts on modes and standards of living:

- Nutritional: cultivating most of our food will limit our intake of dangerous industrial products, leaving us in control of our diets and enabling us to be more conscious of and responsible for our health.

- Social: permaculture is best followed as a community practice so that waste is further reduced through collective consumption and production, according to the specific needs of participants. It also flourishes in the promotion of social cohesion, strengthening human relationships.

- Economic and financial: it is a tremendously efficient way to save money that would otherwise be spent on things that we can create naturally and with little effort, even in the comfort of our homes.

- Political: a people who cultivate most of their own food, harness most of their own energy naturally and depend more on their environment than on the economy and government policies, are a people less affected by poor governance and political instability.

- Environmental: it helps preserve the environment, allowing for natural ecosystems to evolve on their own terms, and to our advantage.

The holistic method of living proposed by permaculture is fun to practice, and is extensively beneficial on all aspects of human development and sustainable environmental management. Through its synergistic collaboration with nature and natural principles it tackles the many dangers of the capitalist system, notably, overproduction and overexploitation of natural resources, waste, and ostentatious consumerism. Permaculture embraces a new and better order of things for an economy of bliss.

CHAPTER SIX

ECONOMICS OF BLISS

Practised correctly, the recommendations of chapter four and of this book as a whole will create for us what should be considered an *Economy of Bliss* or *Happiness*. A little explanation perhaps is necessitated in order to sync it with the foregoing.

The Economics of Bliss is the sustained act of directing one's energy and efforts towards the creation of *Shared Value* in all its forms. Simply put, it means creating wealth by investing physical capital as well as being effectively altruistic, doing good, being socially entrepreneurial, being environmentally conscious, a creator of *Shared Value,* and being able to identify, create and give importance to *real* value, rather than working squarely for money. Engaging in an *Economy of Bliss* rather than a capitalist economy will generate greater productivity and procure for the individuals sustained states of joy. The mindset of dependence on regular jobs will be curtailed in order to empower a lot more people to follow their own dreams and realize them, the fact being that dreams followed are the sine qua non source of fulfilment.

Working in the current global system of pure capitalism has never been fulfilling for everybody. At best, good pay packages come, but scarce senses of career fulfilment or dream realization. Less appealing is that most of the time, even those who love their jobs are poorly paid, whereas in an *Economy of Bliss*, nobody would create value and be unable to make ends meet. In it, no creative expense of valuable energy is ever wasted.

Searching hard and wide for a job, working for a salary, generating profits for invisible men at the top, measuring all productivity in figures and completely ignoring the humanity of those involved, their feelings – are the hallmarks of our current society. The complete opposite characterizes an *Economy of Bliss* in which, unbelievably, there is zero unemployment in the first place, besides abundance of possibilities to work for all kinds of value (not just money), creating value for every member of society (not just for a tiny class of people), working to emancipate oneself and to achieve full potential as a person and (not just to earn for your boss a better-looking balance sheet at the end of the year). In the Economy of Bliss, people, ethics, the environment, the person, etc. matter more.

It is easy to be dismissive and to explain away this as idealistic and not pragmatic or achievable in the real world. But that is exactly where it starts for that is how sceptics also thought of capitalism itself at its genesis. The Industrial Revolution was not considered possible before it took centre stage. Sceptics suggested that the Gold Standard could not be abolished, but it is the FIAT that prevails today; others have suggested that cryptocurrencies are not feasible, but these are gaining unexpected momentum and from the look of things, they will be the reality of marketing in no distant future. Practically, we are left with the simple choice: whether to invest in an *Economy of Bliss* or not to do so. Excuses do not explain away the advantages detailed herein.

The flaunted development through the capitalist system is nothing compared to that which is attainable in an *Economy of Bliss,* characterized by *shared value creation, permaculture, Sharing and gift economies, effective altruism* and *compassion.* The catalogue thus runs to positive infinities:
- equal opportunities,
- limited social injustice,
- increased integration,

- reduced economic oppression due to a fall in the value of money,
- sustainable exploitation of natural resources,
- no extreme poverty,
- no unemployment,
- reduced sickness,
- reduced pollution,
- reduced depression, if any,
- reduced crime,
- ∞

One day at a time, one person at a time, one community at a time, we can move into a new era, one in which value is bartered for value and money used only in rare situations where *shared value* may be difficult to create.

Money and Unemployment

The capitalist's excessive reliance on money is the virus in the system, its sin, a fundamental flaw in its configuration. It is the root cause of the illusions of poverty and unemployment, as well as the cause of a great many of the vices in society: burglary, fraud, corruption, etc. There is a lot of work to be done in the world but lots of people stay idle in the name of unemployment.

Their bugbear is the capitalist platform, which informs their stance, namely, that there is nobody to pay them in cash for the value they may create. If I walk to my neighbour's house and offer to mow the lawn in exchange for a few fruits from her/his orchard, I would have worked and been paid for it, thereby creating *Shared Value*. If I provide consultancy services to a successful entrepreneur in exchange for his mentorship of my aspiring son, I would have created *Shared Value*. If I volunteer at a job in exchange for a recommendation for an opportunity or an extra accreditation in my Curriculum Vitae, I would have created *Shared Value*. There are literally billions of ways we can create value in this manner.

The insistence on getting cash for virtually every single effort made is a huge limitation to progress in a culture that actually favours only a small group of people – the currency minters at the top of the globalized capitalist system. Evidently, poverty and unemployment are kept in place not only by the system, but also by a pathetic lack of knowledge and insight in too many people. In an *Economy of Bliss*, poverty would not mean lack of money but rather lack of knowledge and values such as altruism, courage, creativity and empathy.

One significant pointer often missed out on is the fact that the rich actually trade amongst themselves mostly in terms of value, and not in terms of money. They develop ideas and create coalitions and organizations to execute those ideas. Added to this, they create money and hire people into their companies to invest their value in ideas and skills. To these workers they give a regular but limited supply of money to keep the wheel turning.

It is hard to blame the workers for choosing to work for the limiting money. They are conscripted from a tender age into the indoctrination of dependence on money and the crumbs of value which those at the top are enjoying *for free*. We must think for ourselves and learn to question issues incisively and courageously. Fear must be banished in this endeavour.

Fear

Fear stunts the economic, social and political development of many. We are highly creative beings, with the capacity for all sorts of things, but most people stay conformingly inactive throughout their lives, fearing judgement, change, rejection, poverty, failure, injury, etc. This paralyzes and prevents them from exploring and exploiting their true abilities as they ought to.

Fear thus induces under-exploitation of capabilities and urges evil deeds in the process of obtaining the resources we need to keep us safe from the things we fear. Fear of failure, for example, causes people to cheat and to do nothing when they must act. Fear of lack causes people to steal from others and to hoard resources that would be more useful in different contexts than theirs. Fear of rejection makes people pretend, becoming pseudo personalities and inauthentic in a manner that devastates any form of integrity in them. Fear of judgement causes people to lie and conceal the truth, etc. Moral poverty, thus results essentially from fear. The quaint and apparent simplification of the reality is that moral poverty is the only kind of poverty possible in an *Economy of Bliss*.

People have a lot more opportunities to create value and a wider variety of ways in which to express themselves and their abilities in an *Economy of Bliss*. This reduces the incidence of fear and ensures a more progressive and cohesive society. Recall, as we earlier saw, that a network of good relationships with people and the environment is far more important for survival and growth, than money and material possessions ever can be. Accumulating resources may be good for survival, but it is risky to miss out on the fact that these resources only have value in the context of good relationships with the people around us. In the event of a crisis, law and morals are relegated in favour of survival instincts. Accumulation of resources is a make-shift measure for crisis not a value of proper living. On their own, accumulated resources do not instil security or even comfort. It is the ambiance of the community that can guarantee secure comfort, for in the midst of people who lack basic needs, the well-provided-for rich man hangs on the cliff of uncertainty, making his accumulated resources a source of pain to himself and others.

Business and Money

Most companies struggle to look virtuous in their commercials through even fanciful initiatives of corporate social responsibility. They spend a lot of advertising money to sugar-coat sometimes poisonous products by video commercials, images and slogans that suggest real value, appealing to our emotions. They act or mimic tapping from the value in an *Economy of Bliss*, but for purely capitalist motives.

In an *Economy of Bliss,* business is strictly social entrepreneurship and the elevated practice of barter in an atmosphere that creates shared value. The incidence of money is reduced and its impact weakened. Hinged to this, negative practices carried out to accumulate money in the capitalist system naturally fade away. People in such a setup work for various causes but get paid their dues more in kind than in cash. For example, you may create a local social enterprise dealing in hygiene and sanitation, and offer your services to a restaurant, a school, a clothing store and a transportation company. In return you will get paid with a daily supply of food from the restaurant, tuition for your children, clothing and transportation.

The culture of money has infected our minds so thoroughly that we virtually equate money with the air we breathe. But money has been nothing more than promissory pieces of paper which facilitate trade. Today, it is backed by nothing more than the trust of those who use it – all of us – even though most people have no clue where it comes from, how it is controlled and by whom.

Most of the world economy is at the mercy of the Federal Reserve Bank of America, which is a privately-owned bank that prints the dollars used all over the world. These bankers would print a fixed amount of money from thin air and lend it to the government and to private borrowers at an interest, then print more money to lend to more borrowers as the first borrowers are repaying their debt. These entrepreneurs then obtain value from naïve people in exchange for the dollar that they have been trained to both fear and trust so much. The values so obtained makes these business people ostentatiously comfortable; their elite bankers are even more comfortable at the expense of those brainwashed to give away their sense of true value in exchange for dollar bills.

The true beneficiaries of the capitalist system are those at the top who control the money. Those who work for money are victims of the system, no matter how sour that sounds. Most of those who put in intense work hours and create real value are underpaid for the services rendered, and they feel incapable of doing anything about it. So, they force themselves to put up with the injustice and to work even harder in order to acquire the money of their dreams. Most of the time, the riches they dream about never catch up with them in their lifetime. The *Economy of Bliss* is a golden opportunity to escape this web of poverty and social injustice, spun around well-meaning but ignorant human beings.

Relationships

It has been iterated enough that relationships are the main source of value in an *Economy of Bliss*. It takes much effort and sacrifice for two parties to build a lasting, profitable relationship, and the effort invested therein is never wasted. Money in the capitalist system, on the other hand, can be lost in a failed investment. As upheld in the World Bank's study, *"Where is the Wealth of Nations"*, most of the wealth of a nation lies in the values shared by its people. Empirically, a set of healthy relationships with virtuous people is more valuable than the world's money and is the only possible way to achieve a life of abundance.

There is tremendous potential in the relationships you nurture with the people around you. This potential can only be unleashed by managing these relationships with proper care. Managing a relationship properly does not require so much time and attention but valuable input such as honesty, reliability, integrity and, constant giving as in the gift economy. Giving time and attention every now and then, especially when it is needed, offering gifts, complements, advice, constructive and supportive criticism are the makings and the key in relationships.

The celebrated Indian spiritual leader, Swami Vivekananda, has said that "Relationships are more important than life, but it is important for those relationships to have life in them." He juggles the vitality of relationships with the need for them to be dynamic. In practice, the happiest and most successful people in the world, purposefully trade in value, not because they do not like money or that they have too much of it, but because they know that the relationships they build and the value they exchange in these relationships, will always be more important than money. The relationships we nurture are the whole essence of who we are in society at any point in time.

The alliterated musicality of the Zulu proverb *"Umuntu ngumuntu ngabantu"* which has been highly popularized literally translates as *"a person is a person through other people"*. The same rhythmic echo and meaning reverberates in the phrase *"Wir dze wir bi' wir"* of the Nso language of the North West Region of Cameroon. The logic is that, no matter what social rungs one mounts, his or her value is only guaranteed in the recognition of his affinity with others, which comes in his/her relationship with them. Literally, therefore, the value of a person comes from relating with other persons.

The logicality of this perception expands into a virtual law. If you despise a person now, you put your own self at risk. No one masters the twists and turns of fate for every person you come in contact with, is a potential step on the ladder to your greatest desires. You, too, are a step on the success ladder of others. Life in this respect is one big *njangi* as the local parlance holds it, in the term which defines a rotating savings and credit association. One *njangi* rule is: if you fail to contribute today, you will not be credited tomorrow.

Yet, some relationships could be toxic to growth since not everybody can be the same and even if an *Economy of Bliss* were fully achieved, we would still have negative people in society. While we try our bests not to be the bad seed in a relationship, it is nonetheless wise to avoid negative people. This avoidance, however, should not come from mere prejudice. You must plant a good seed and give it time to grow, repeating the process every now and then, whenever you encounter the purported negative people. At all cost, you must protect yourself from negative influence, but it is of higher value to influence negativity positively. Just as a worthwhile business must offer value to its customers and pay its owners in cash, a good relationship must, sooner or later, bring value to both parties.

It is often at old age that people make deep retrospective assessments of their lives, and it is then also that they reap the fruits of their lifelong labour. At this stage and age, they best understand the importance of certain values neglected in youth as well as mistakes planted in the past. How happy or unhappy we feel then depends on the extent to which we invested our personal economies with altruism and gratitude, the extent to which our personal economies actually became *Economies of Bliss*.

Poverty and Poor People

There may be crises like hunger, drought, natural or man-made disasters, but financial poverty is not a crisis. It is only an artificial concept like currency. So, those who label themselves "poor" for lack of money, only display ignorance. Money is a means to an end, not an end in itself. This means that an illusion of lack is created by focusing on it and its scarcity. The idea of poverty reflects our misconception of value.

In an *Economy of Bliss*, people deal with each other in terms of value, not money. Poverty in that case only features in terms of real value – lack of creativity, knowledge, courage, etc. There will always be a way to create value to share, and to offer in exchange for the value needed to sustain oneself. It soon filters to the laughable fact that poor people in the current system are those who envy the lives of those who fuel and control the capitalist system. They accuse their lack of money for their inability to live the kind of life they desire. This is exactly the ignorance that maintains the mindset of most people in poverty.

The rich, by contrast, know how to take responsibility and do not shy away from it. They know that the more responsibilities one has, the bigger one grows, as acknowledging responsibilities is what moves people to action, and action is the core of progress. Progress, in turn, is the central piece in the collection of values that constitute success. A person running away from responsibility is like a car which does not move, and therefore does not fulfil its purpose. Such a static object or person does not deserve the resources for activity, health and even life. He/she/it depreciates morally and expires quickly.

If we relate the saying – "a rolling stone gathers no moss" to work, the meaning crystalizes in that if you keep working, you will not gather moss nor catch rust like an unused engine. If you face your responsibilities and act on them with the value mindset, your personal economy will grow in size and value.

Thinking in terms of service is all it takes to move you from poverty to abundance. If you reserve the ability to think and you have your hands and legs in place, you can always change your situation with a simple action. You can quit being bitter about life and choose to be grateful and happy at your current state and then go on to building from where you are. Think of what you can do "for free" rather than being idle from "unemployment" or poverty.

That is how value is created, which in turn creates opportunities.

The power of giving deals with proportions and not aggregates. You don't need the world's energy or excessive resources to give service, a thing captured in the biblical story of the widow's might. To be hidden and idle is a way of making the spirit bitter, it is like letting the milk go sour from long non-use or neglect, for there is always somebody you can assist in something. Doing this with a joyful heart swells your personal networks and adds value to you as a person. It can lead to permanent perspective and life changes. It is therefore recommended for each person to try developing an outgoing character and to become as useful or helpful as possible to others.

Everybody has more than enough of something to be shared with those who may need more of that thing. No resource is meant to be idle – money, time, attention. If nobody will buy it, then give it out to whoever may need it more than you, rather than keeping it idle. Make this a habit, a way of life. You will benefit more from the gratitude of the receiver than you will from stockpiling idle resources. The gratitude of others is a greater force than is often thought and, joined to altruistic networks of people, it is what powers the *Economy of Bliss,* the economy which produces long life and happiness.

One sure way to realize that you have reasons to be happy is by momentarily directing your interest to the troubles of the people around you. Set out a day or time to listen to other people, even if you cannot solve their problems. Give an attentive ear, listening to others and try to understand them while offering them advice or encouragement according to your resources and where necessary. This way, you ease their burden at the same time as you build up your relationship with them. So-disposed, when you realize that everyone has their mountain to climb, yours will become a little lighter.

Generating Abundance

"...the richest 85 people across the globe share a combined wealth of £1tn, as much as the poorest 3.5 billion of the world's population..." – **The Guardian Newspaper, October 2014.**

Although nobody is really entitled to anything on earth, we all reserve the right to enjoy the beauty of the world in all its expanse, to savour all the gifts and riches of nature, the children and keepers of which we all happen to be. In the capitalist tradition, these natural rights have been debased and privatized; price tags have been attached to things whose value we really cannot measure in monetary terms. The idea that sustained wealth and comfort cannot be acquired by focusing on accumulating capital or lamenting over material poverty and asking the 'rich' to share their wealth, comes in here. For while destitution is real, it must be seen as little more than the manifestation of a way of life and thought which can be changed at will. It can be reversed by operating in an *Economy of Bliss*.

Investing true value into your future to experience the beautifully addictive feeling of blissful abundance is hidden in the following scarce knowledge and perception: dream honourably and work hard towards your goals without enviously comparing yourself and your success with anyone else's, but rather seeking at every available opportunity to lend a helping hand towards the success of another, to participate. Experience immediate and eventual fulfilment by investing true value into your future. The rewards of such a lifestyle will be reaped not only by yourself but also by your offspring and later generations.

Every thought of gratitude or appreciation directed at you for your good works affects your surrounding as well; the gratitude you also express for the blessings you enjoy are a source of power and energy which we should not ignore. People with good public reputation are capable of great influence and the ability to create wealth. If you should reflect for a brief moment, you would certainly identify someone whose interest you are ready to defend even in their absence, should you ever have the opportunity. Now, imagine having not one, but multitudes of people thinking the same of you.

The more we recognize our individual progress, benefits and advantages and qualify them as absolute rather than comparative, the happier, healthier and more productive we get. The feeling of fulfilment in surpassing oneself is a lot greater than any benefits we can get in trying to surpass others. Synergy rather than rivalry is what counts. And symbiotic collaboration is in the nature of human beings to practise, being a highly productive kind of relationship between two things. Rivalry and negative competition are quite obviously counter-productive and this is the atmosphere of capitalistic competition. Untold damage ensues, since it is difficult to calculate the consequences of our crushing actions and putdown attitudes on third party stakeholders in such rabid activities. In capitalistic mutual elbowing, the desire to win almost always has the upper hand over the desire to be ethical and of sound integrity.

To return to the effect of giving, gratitude or appreciation may be expressed or not. Either ways, so long as it is felt, free-giving is a powerful investment. Expressed sincere gratitude is also an investment for he who does so as it secures more good things to the grateful as well as more reasons to be grateful. It is a feeling I am familiar with, and it can be pleasantly addictive, driving away worry and making one sustainably happy if it is made a habit.

This doping feeling explains why some people cannot help but give whenever the opportunity presents itself. *Tenpercent Africa* has imbibed this value in which a network of people has been that grows each day with examples of people living in abundance, having understood the philosophy of happiness and plenty. It is not how much they give in to material oblivion that drives their passion, but how much wealth they create by giving.

The privy of gratitude-conscious people is that the universe is designed and run through with more happiness following open unhesitating appreciation. How much one lacks is a function of how much one appreciates what one already has. Those who are always thankful in their hearts and express it with their mouths, those who do not focus on what they do not have, these are the people who eventually get everything they need.

The power of a culture of giving and gratitude to produce a sense of abundance is thus as real as any other proven physical law, especially visible when several people are in a network. Having a multitude of people think good of you is an achievement, and their willingness to return to you a well-deserved good deed at any time you may need it, is fulfilment. This fulfilment represents the end result of your act of kindness.

The Mental Wellbeing Loop

Scientific studies abound in proof of the fact that positive effects follow the practising of an economy of bliss, such as gratitude and free-giving. Neuroscience has it that the orbital frontal cortex is the part of the brain which controls emotions. It thrives on healthy relationships in which values such as honesty and trust abound. These conditions permit the orbital frontal cortex to develop properly, giving us the ability to manage our emotions and to endow us with a greater tendency towards emotional intelligence.

Emotional intelligence is the kind of intelligence we apply to maintain peace and mutual understanding, thereby building strong relationships with people of any nature. These strong relationships then provide better and better conditions for the development of the orbital frontal cortex, which further empowers us to build more and stronger relationships, as well as more possibilities to create wealth. This keeps us in a virtuous loop as illustrated below.

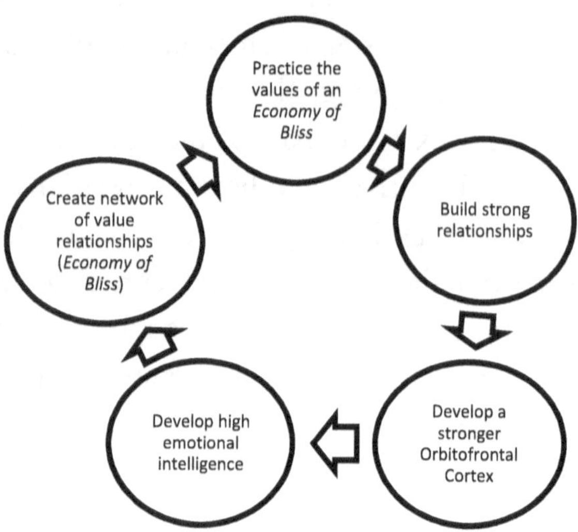

In addition to the virtuous mental wellbeing loop of the *Economy of Bliss*, and in line with the principles of Causality and dynamic equilibrium, those who fail to exercise a certain degree of altruistic thinking and action find it difficult to integrate themselves fully in society. They find it difficult to make the necessary human connections to facilitate progress in any social endeavour. They also tend to have less options for their personal development than altruistic people do. Besides, they are often overwhelmed by feelings of insecurity, feeling undeserving and unworthy. Some cannot even participate publicly in society.

Altruistic people, on the other hand, whether introverted or extroverted in character, tend to have a valuable network of friends and acquaintances. It is a general character trait of most successful people that they know how to give value to other people and things.

Joy Today, Tomorrow Secured

The capacity for empathy is controlled by the prefrontal cortex which, when damaged or under-activated, develops antisocial and impulsive behaviour. The person loses links with purposeful behaviour, no longer able to pursue any virtuously creative ambition. A conclusive implication of this is that empathy is a prerequisite for self-realization, a prerequisite for joy. For joy comes with the sustained feeling of progression in life, erasing any overflow of worry about your future.

Worry about rainy days that are likely to freeze today's unneeded resources for the next year is a normal and rational practice. From this, it stands to reason that there is wisdom in being cautious of the uncertainty factor only for the person who has failed to build a reliable network of healthy relationships in the course of their lives. For no matter the level of precautions we take in view of rainy days, life remains precarious.

In Cameroon, it is often said by job seekers that "connections are more important than certificates" and indeed the wisdom carries further, for relationships are more important than possessions, a dictum that validly applies virtually everywhere. Investing in relationships brings the kind of security that cannot be procured with money and riches. It provides a sense of security which resonates from within and which does not depend on any external party. It takes away worry and brings joy, making the individual extra confident about their future. He or she spends time planting seeds in hearts rather than on stones or money for that matter.

Worrying about the future is the sure way to be unhappy now and always. It drains you of vital energy and slowly but surely takes away the life in you. Famous ancient Greek philosopher, Aristotle, is quoted as saying, "What is the essence of life? It is to serve others and to do good." Biblical references in this regard abound, particularly from the lips of Jesus about storing up treasure in heaven (persons) rather than on rust-prone money, not worrying about tomorrow, the wily servant who creates relationships to save himself when he loses his master's trust and job, etc.

It is enriching to cultivate a habit of connecting regularly with people and sharing value. Even in a society as fiercely capitalist as ours, the most important form of wealth is to be loved and appreciated by as many people as possible through the love and appreciation we also give out. This is the proven greatest assurance for tomorrow. For about 80 years, a Harvard University study was made on the ultimate determinant of a fulfilling old age. An article on this study, written by Liz Mineo for the Harvard official online gazette is found in the annex at the end of this book.

Network into Economic Bliss

We have fully consolidated the fact that in order to get the most value out of life, we must become socially responsible, striving always to give more; that an economy which depends strictly on money, runs many risks, including man-made disasters like widespread anarchy and violation of basic human rights, due especially to the inequality problems. These cannot exist in an *Economy of Bliss*, for the value there is not in money or things but in the characters and collective actions of people with value networks.

An economic transition from the purely capitalist system is near-impossible without the oppressive intervention of corrupted states against their weaker populations. The rich will seek to preserve their money and power by all means at the expense of innocent lives at the bottom of the pyramid. To create the kind of value needed for an eventual smooth economic transition, people must begin to detach themselves from money. Making financial investments to secure a regular cashflow should go on, but exchanging more value in your relationship networks should be given pride of place over money.

Create *Shared Value* Groups in which you share valuables like clothing and food with each other. Emphasis needs to move from the creation of economic value to the creation of human/social value. Only by harnessing the potential of social value can economic sustainability be achieved, given that social value is largely underrated in economics; it deserves more academic and practical attention, being the basic fabric of any society. It allows that society to operate in an organized manner, enabling commerce and economic activities. As it stands, a big shift in mindset and habits, is the only way the errors of pure capitalistic thinking may be corrected, the only way a peaceful and sustainable economic transition may be guaranteed us, or our children.

A story in *The Beauty of Charity* by Ahmed Ali al-Kuwaity reiterates the value of altruism, thus:

Sayyid Husayn Muddarrisi relates that one of his female relatives had seen his dead father in a dream. His father's face was illuminating with light and beside him was a woman who was folding beautiful and smart clothes the likes of which she had never seen in this world before. When asked where the clothes had come from, the woman replied that they were for his father and that they had been sent by his sons for him. This woman who had seen the dream asked all his dead father's relatives whether they had done any special good deeds for their father. One of the Sayyid's brothers was taken aback and admit-

ted that he had prepared for some clothes to be given to orphans but he had not actually distributed them. The Sayyid was so surprised to know that a deed had been rewarded when only a decision was made on his part and the charitable act had not taken place yet. So, this suggests that any charitable act done for the dead reaches them immediately, as soon as you make the intention.

Although wrapped in myth and somewhat fanciful, this parabolic representation of how an altruistic action can carry is authentic. The ancients prized the act of sharing as noble and identified complete detachment from material possessions as the way to achieve absolute happiness. This virtue underlies one of the vows taken by religious orders or congregations – the vow of poverty. By this vow, the religious monk or nun shares in the provisions of his or her community but undertakes to own nothing personal.

It is hoped that the writing of this book will both starts up and help to implant a system of *Shared Value* groups to merge and create open-source community development projects where people will provide quality voluntary service and goods to realize a common social cause, producing value based on their collective interests as a community.

Tenpercent Africa is a network of this kind, a growing community of socially responsible free-givers, effectively utilizing input from volunteers and experts from all walks of life. The goal is to realize projects for collective development, help the poor and needy, save and make the environment more beautiful and habitable. *Tenpercent* echoes the biblical tithing principle of *ten percent* and the one of ten lepers who returned to give thanks for being cleansed. *Tenpercent Africa* encourages people to participate with ten percent, not only of their money, but of their time and knowledge to develop their communities and to harness the power and widespread practice of collective social responsibility. Constructive activities, such as community labour, sensitization, teaching, vocational training, mentorship etc. are avenues for this practice.

Starting with You

At this point, the assumption is that the reader has understood or gained consciousness of the fact that beyond all the economic policies and social welfare systems that govern the world, we are individually accountable for the welfare of our nearest neighbours and immediate environment. That the reader has also gained consciousness of the fact that it is a duty to share value in order to keep society, the environment and ecosystems stable and in natural harmony.

Just as nobody knows it all, nobody has it all. By sharing and exchanging knowledge and resources, people progress. The state of an economy, whether booming or stagnating, is not a function of how much money is exchanged but of how much value is exchanged. Money must therefore not be a limitation on value exchange.

Chances are that there is something of greater value in the hands of one person, and that someone else somewhere else also has something which might be much more useful to you than it is to them. This thing might be material, skill, information, or ideas. The goal is to make every resource available for the creation of value. In a state and tradition of perpetual exchange of value we can all get the things we need, and when we need them. When one restrains from giving out useful information or from giving away something which they do not need, they miss the opportunity to create and share value and to properly allocate resources for increased ecological productivity to make the world more sustainable.

The reader can access the *Tenpercent Africa Organization* to become

- A *builder*, providing resources and voluntary service to contribute effectively to the building of communities.

- A *Shared Value broker*, generating real value and facilitating the exchange of value around you.

- A *philanthropist*, dedicating part of your life to doing good for others and providing them with hope and opportunities for a better life.

- An *environmentalist*, protecting the environment in which we live and militating for its protection by other stakeholders.

- A *contributor* to and beneficiary of an *Economy of Bliss,* sharing in the ever-growing value pool of the large Tenpercent Africa network.

- Become a *Tenpercenter*, a new person with a refreshing perspective to life; one with more creative activity, more colour, more friendship, more goodness, and more humanity.

EPILOGUE

This book is the expression of my desire to bring more people to acknowledge the fact that they have the ability to do a lot more than they think they can, to make the world a better place; that they can do this by generating happiness and satisfaction through creating and sharing value, and in one voice, getting every individual in the world to know, and to acknowledge that they have something to offer; that they always have something to give and everything to be grateful for; that there is always somebody on whose face they can put a smile and receive one in return, somebody to whom reason might be given to say thank you, even if they don't, and somebody in whom to plant a seed which will yield sweet memory. To

163

the joy of that somebody, they can attach themselves as good thoughts travel all the way from them in prayer. The joy of being responsible for someone's happiness every day is unspeakable.

The world has drifted away from the reality that we are all interconnected with one another, that the energy which animates all of us is of ultimate singularity; that for the whole to be healthy, the parts must all be healthy. Development also, especially in Africa, has been greatly stalled by this lack of collectivism and collaboration, and mounted a low sense of responsibility on layers of the social scale. This mentality is a basic cause of many socio-political and economic shortcomings.

It is hoped that with the publication of this book, the foundation of the Social Enterprise, the *Tenpercent Africa Organization* dedicated to bringing populations together from the base, will be better known and that more and more people will volunteer to contribute their time, resources and personal effort to rebuild society for good.

By reading this book and practicing its content, you fuel the hope of a better society, and as in the rice experiment, our thoughts of gratitude will uplift you in many ways.

Umuntu ngumuntu ngabantu.
Wir dze wir bi' wir.

ANNEX

The Nearly Eighty-Year-Old Harvard Study on Happiness

Good genes are nice, but joy is better. *Harvard study, almost 80 years old proves that embracing community helps us live longer and be happier.*

Article by Liz Mineo, Harvard Staff Writer.

When scientists began tracking the health of 268 Harvard sophomores in 1938 during the Great Depression, they hoped the longitudinal study would reveal clues to leading healthy and happy lives. They got more than they wanted.

After following the surviving Crimson men for nearly 80 years as part of the Harvard Study of Adult Development, one of the world's longest studies of adult life, researchers have collected a cornucopia of data on their physical and mental health.

Of the original Harvard cohort recruited as part of the Grant Study, only 19 are still alive, all in their mid-90s. Among the original recruits were eventual President John F. Kennedy and long-time Washington Post editor Ben Bradlee. (Women weren't in the original study because the College was still all-male.)

In addition, scientists eventually expanded their research to include the men's offspring, who now number 1,300 and are in their 50s and 60s, to find out how early-life experiences affect health and aging over time. Some participants went on to become successful businessmen, doctors, lawyers, while others ended up as schizophrenics or alcoholics, but not on inevitable tracks.

During the intervening decades, the control groups have expanded. In the 1970s, 456 Boston inner-city residents were enlisted as part of the Glueck Study, and 40 of them are still alive. More than a decade ago, researchers began including wives in the Grant and Glueck studies.

Over the years, researchers have studied the participants' health trajectories and their broader lives, including their triumphs and failures in careers and marriage, and the findings have produced startling lessons, and not only for the researchers.

"The surprising finding is that our relationships and how happy we are in our relationships has a powerful influence on our health," said Robert Waldinger, director of the study, a psychiatrist at Massachusetts General Hospital and a professor of psychiatry at Harvard Medical School. "Taking care of your body is important, but tending to your relationships is a form of self-care too. That, I think, is the revelation."

Close relationships, more than money or fame, are what keep people happy throughout their lives, the study revealed. Those ties protect people from life's discontents, help to delay mental and physical decline, and are better predictors of long and happy lives than social class, IQ, or even genes. That finding proved true across the board among both the Harvard men and the inner-city participants.

The long-term research has received funding from private foundations, but has been financed largely by grants from the National Institutes of Health, first through the National Institute of Mental Health, and more recently through the National Institute on Aging.

Researchers who have pored through data, including vast medical records and hundreds of in-person interviews and questionnaires, found a strong correlation between men's flourishing lives and their relationships with family, friends, and community. Several studies found that people's level of satisfaction with their relationships at age 50 was a better predictor of physical health than their cholesterol levels were.

"When we gathered together everything we knew about them at age 50, it wasn't their middle-age cholesterol levels that predicted how they were going to grow old," said Waldinger in a popular TED Talk. "It was how satisfied they were in their relationships. The people who were the most satisfied in their relationships at age 50 were the healthiest at age 80."

He recorded his TED talk, titled "What Makes a Good Life? Lessons from the Longest Study on Happiness," in 2015, and it has been viewed 13,000,000 times.

The researchers also found that marital satisfaction has a protective effect on people's mental health. Part of a study found that people who had happy marriages in their 80s reported that their moods didn't suffer even on the days when they had more physical pain. Those who had unhappy marriages felt both more emotional and physical pain.

Those who kept warm relationships got to live longer and happier, said Waldinger, and the loners often died earlier. "Loneliness kills," he said. "It's as powerful as smoking or alcoholism."

According to the study, those who lived longer and enjoyed sound health avoided smoking and alcohol in excess. Researchers also found that those with strong social support experienced less mental deterioration as they aged.

In part of a recent study, researchers found that women who felt securely attached to their partners were less depressed and happier in their relationships two-and-a-half years later, and also had better memory functions than those with frequent marital conflicts.

"Good relationships don't just protect our bodies; they protect our brains," said Waldinger in his TED talk. "And those good relationships, they don't have to be smooth all the time. Some of our octogenarian couples could bicker with each other day in and day out, but as long as they felt that they could really count on the other when the going got tough, those arguments didn't take a toll on their memories."

Since aging starts at birth, people should start taking care of themselves at every stage of life, the researchers say.

"Aging is a continuous process," Waldinger said. "You can see how people can start to differ in their health trajectory in their 30s, so that by taking good care of yourself early in life you can set yourself on a better course for aging. The best advice I can give is 'Take care of your body as though you were going to need it for 100 years,' because you might."

The study, like its remaining original subjects, has had a long life, spanning four directors, whose tenures reflected their medical interests and views of the time.

Under the first director, Clark Heath, who stayed from 1938 until 1954, the study mirrored the era's dominant view of genetics and biological determinism. Early researchers believed that physical constitution, intellectual ability, and personality traits determined adult development. They made detailed anthropometric measurements of skulls, brow bridges, and moles, wrote in-depth notes on the functioning of major organs, examined brain activity through electroencephalograms, and even analysed the men's handwriting.

Now, researchers draw men's blood for DNA testing and put them into MRI scanners to examine organs and tissues in their bodies, procedures that would have sounded like science fiction back in 1938. In that sense, the study itself represents a history of the changes that life brings.

Psychiatrist George Vaillant, who joined the team as a researcher in 1966, led the study from 1972 until 2004. Trained as a psychoanalyst, Vaillant emphasized the role of relationships, and came to recognize the crucial role they played in people living long and pleasant lives.

In a book called "Aging Well," Vaillant wrote that six factors predicted healthy aging for the Harvard men: physical activity, absence of alcohol abuse and smoking, having mature mechanisms to cope with life's ups and downs, and enjoying both a healthy weight and a stable marriage. For the inner-city men, education was an additional factor. "The more education the inner city men obtained," wrote Vaillant, "the more likely they were to stop smoking, eat sensibly, and use alcohol in moderation."

Vaillant's research highlighted the role of these protective factors in healthy aging. The more factors the subjects had in place, the better the odds they had for longer, happier lives.

"When the study began, nobody cared about empathy or attachment," said Vaillant. "But the key to healthy aging is relationships, relationships, relationships."

The study showed that the role of genetics and long-lived ancestors proved less important to longevity than the level of satisfaction with relationships in midlife, now recognized as a good predictor of healthy aging. The research also debunked the idea that people's personalities "set like plaster" by age 30 and cannot be changed.

"Those who were clearly train wrecks when they were in their 20s or 25s turned out to be wonderful octogenarians," he said. "On the other hand, alcoholism and major depression could take people who started life as stars and leave them at the end of their lives as train wrecks."

The study's fourth director, Waldinger has expanded research to the wives and children of the original men. That is the second-generation study, and Waldinger hopes to expand it into the third and fourth generations. "It will probably never be replicated," he said of the lengthy research, adding that there is yet more to learn.

"We're trying to see how people manage stress, whether their bodies are in a sort of chronic 'fight or flight' mode," Waldinger said. "We want to find out how it is that a difficult childhood reaches across decades to break down the body in middle age and later."

Lara Tang '18, a human and evolutionary biology concentrator who recently joined the team as a research assistant, relishes the opportunity to help find some of those answers. She joined the effort after coming across Waldinger's TED talk in one of her classes.

"That motivated me to do more research on adult development," said Tang. "I want to see how childhood experiences affect developments of physical health, mental health, and happiness later in life."

Asked what lessons he has learned from the study, Waldinger, who is a Zen priest, said he practices meditation daily and invests time and energy in his relationships, more than before.

"It's easy to get isolated, to get caught up in work and not remembering, 'Oh, I haven't seen these friends in a long time,'" Waldinger said. "So, I try to pay more attention to my relationships than I used to."

Echoes from My Coaching Network

As a personal development coach, the network I'm building with my clients is a perfect example of a *Shared Value* network. People contact me for my services, which I provide, and along the line we find ourselves looking out for each other and building a value chain, the kind which would be hard to build in the streets on a regular day. Today, coaching is to me no longer a profession or a vocation but an investment. An investment in relationships, in an Economy of Bliss. Some of my friends in my coaching network generously shared their experiences with us. Hopefully, it will lead more people to see the need for a coach and I will in turn expand my value network.

Alake J.:

"Going through crazy situations in life and the inability to freely talk about these issues to someone is quite a horrible phase to go through. Creating space for a life coach in my life has improved the way I view and tackle situations. Yea, you may wonder why you would have to pay money for someone to guide you.

Personally, I got a fear of being judged, even by my own family and friends. And also, the fear of them not giving me their honest opinions because they don't want to hurt my feelings.

To me, a coach is like a medical doctor who will listen to you and not judge, and give you their honest opinions. He thinks with you, suggests guidelines which you may consider or not; it's your choice. In short, he guides and leads you.

It is pure folly to try to change another person to suit you or situations in life. The only person you can change is yourself, and I discovered this through my coach, and I have been quietly changing myself and my way of thinking and handling some issues in life.

I am enjoying this relationship and if you relate to my situation, you should join me.

Arrey M.B.:

I had an emotional problem and for the first time, I solicited the services of a life coach. He gave me a listening ear to everything and came out with possible solutions. He has a way of fitting completely in one's shoes and taking every situation calmly. So, I regained confidence in myself and came out of the depression.

As time went by after my first encounter with my life coach, we began talking of things people can consider "out of place" or weird but he has this magic gift of comprehending every situation and starting a polite and meaningful conversation with his client, and then solutions just present themselves.

Generally, I believe dialogue is very important to humans because through it, we can get to feel or know what our neighbour is going through and more. Talking to an expert or a life coach has really given me confidence in myself, a sense of belonging and a very positive view of things now.

I think there should exist a human library where we can check out humans instead of books and "borrow" persons who have stories to tell from their unique life experiences.

Mambo C.:

At first, I was very uncomfortable and shy opening up to him because I regarded him as a total stranger, but within five minutes of talking to him I felt at home. In the course of our conversation, he listened keenly to all my worries and I found that he is blessed to have experienced many of the problems in which youths find themselves today. He totally understood my problem and did not only help me explain myself better, but he also helped me to better understand the problem I was facing.

He is totally positive, and his positivity lifted up my spirit and helped me understand how little my problem really was. I felt that the problem was already solved, and I was willing to do everything to get out of my situation.

With regard to the solutions he gives, they are quite attainable if you are willing to make a little effort. I saw life from a different perspective, with a thousand reasons to be happy, and many things to do which could bring about my own happiness, irrespective of the way I felt at the moment. He made me see many loopholes in my life, my character and especially my method of handling situations. With his help as a coach, I was positive and ready to face life afresh.

I personally acknowledge the importance of a life coach, as you may have seen from my experience with him. However, I would love to state that most of our problems aggravate because we seek solutions from the wrong places. We confide in persons like us who may become more emotionally involved in our problems than we are, and so give us the wrong solutions. A life coach is an impartial listener who has an insight capable of understanding us without necessarily taking our side. He has the capacity and experience to prove to us that we may be our own very problem. He follows us up till the solution is sought and you are finally up on your own feet. He willingly keeps all your secrets and will help you out with other life matters.

Y.Y.F:

Depression was at its peak and I saw my whole world crumbling when I was betrayed by someone who had made me see no reason to live without him by my side. At one point, it was more of an obsession as the word really means. Being in that state, I never knew I could be strong again, considering how immense the hurt was. I suffered these feelings until I encountered a life coach who showed me a different way of coping with the situation I faced. It was like the best thing that happened to me during that period because he made me understand that the greatest mistake I ever made was to rely on someone for my own happiness...

He gave me tips on how to add value to my life and he inculcated in me a positive spirit which indeed has made my life beautiful again... My life is back to normal and I am happier than ever....

Now, have u been in the same situation, or perhaps felt as if to give up on life? A life coach is the perfect therapy for you and the beauty of your life would be revived again...

Nasima M.:
I have this wonderful professional relationship with my life coach which helps me to produce extraordinary results in my career and business. Life coaching for me, is not counselling or therapy, it is forward looking and it is about achieving positive results in my life. My coach shows me techniques and simple strategies for helping me to close the gap between where I am at and what I want to achieve.

In the time I've had with my coach, I've learned CLARITY. I got clear about what I would achieve from coaching and even my goals became clearer to me. Also, I'm surer about the direction I'm headed in. I've learned ACCOUNTABILITY. This is a powerful tool for creating change. With my coach, we set goals to achieve after every session, both realistic and achievable. And I have to account for the achievement or non-achievement of the goals. Most importantly, I get UNBIASED INPUT from my coach. It makes a big difference to my perspective and helps me see things about my myself and my life situations differently. Your mum might always remind you of your strengths but hearing the same message from someone outside of your situation can be helpful.

Life coaching is an opportunity for me, to focus on my dreams and aspirations. It gives me space to think about me, my thoughts and feelings and about what is important to me. It can be truly life-changing and can enable you to carve the space in your life for your goals and what is important to you. I can boldly say my experience with my life coach has been the best. It has enhanced my personal development and has assisted me in taking various areas of my life to the next level!

****

These people and the many others I interact with, represent my wealth. I give them value, and my value returns to me with a bonus. If I should write another book in the next, say, 20 years' time, I will tell the story of how I shared value with each member of my network, how the knowledge of Shared Value helped them over the years and how my personal relationship with each one of them would have also paved the way for me as they climbed up their various success ladders. Start building your own network!

Some Useful Reads

Arden, B. John. (2010) *Rewire Your Brain*

Bailey, Ronald. (2007) *The Secrets of the Intangible   Wealth.* www.reason.com

BBC. *(*2000*) Africa's Greatest Explorer.*

Benatar, David (2006).*Better Never to Have Been.*

Diawara, Gaoussou. *The Saga of Abubakari 2*

Digdon, Nancy & **Koble**, Amy. (2011). *Effects of Constructive Worry, Imagery Distraction, and Gratitude Interventions on Sleep Quality: A Pilo Trial. Applied Psychology: Health and Wellbeing.* 3. 193-206. 10.1111/j. 1758 0854.2011.01049.x.

Dugas et al. (2016). *Quest for Significance and Sacrifice. Journal of Personality and Social Psychology.* 2003, Vol.84, No 2, 377-389

Kruglanski , Chen, Dechesne, Fishman & Orehek (2014). *Motivation, Ideology and the Social Process in Radicalization.*

Médecins *Québécois pour le Régime Public* (mqrp.qc.ca), 25 February 2018.

Steiner, Rudolf. (2008). *The Four Temperaments.*

"The Psychology of Ownership: Work Environmental Structure, Organizational Commitment and Citizenship Behaviors." *Group and Organization Management.* 31(3):388-416. June 2006.

World Bank. (2006) *Where is the Wealth of Nations? Measuring Capital for the 21st Century.*

Wikipedia en.m.wikipedia.org/wiki/2015_Baltimore_protests

<borgenproject.org/poorest-country-world-democratic-republic-congo>

<en.m.wikipedia.org/wiki/2017-18_Iranian_protests

<guides.library.cornell.edu/c.php?g=31688&p=200750>

<www.effectivealtruism.org/articles/introduction-to-effective-altruism/>

<www.permaculturenews.org/what-is-permaculture/>

<archive.attn.com/stories/1541/baltimore-poverty-facts>